THE LEAN DESIGN SOLUTION

A PRACTICAL GUIDE TO STREAMLINING
PRODUCT DESIGN AND DEVELOPMENT

BART HUTHWAITE

INSTITUTE FOR LEAN DESIGN
MACKINAC ISLAND, MICHIGAN
2004

The Lean Design Solution
Copyright 2004 by Bart Huthwaite

Institute for Lean Design
9 French Outpost
P.O. Box 1999
Mackinac Island, MI 49757

906-847-6094
info@leandesign.org
www.leandesign.org

ISBN 0-9712210-2-2

Second Printing

Manufactured in the United States of America

Cover and interior design and layout by
Words Plus Design, 888-883-8347
www.wordsplusdesign.com

Contents

This book is dedicated to…

All the thousands of product development teams and individuals who have generously shared their thinking with me
over the years. Thank you for the opportunity to share your
thoughts with others.

And…

My wife Nina, daughter Heather and son Bart Huthwaite, Jr.
whose constant support and creative ideas made this
book possible.

Preface

This is a "How To" book. The *Lean Design Solution* is a tightly-knit set of tools, techniques and methods for creating products with more value and less waste.

You will learn step-by-step how to design *"lean"* products and services.

This book will also show you how to "design in" Six Sigma quality.

Applying the *Lean Design Solution* process will help you achieve better profits, greater sales, entry to new markets, and lower company-wide costs.

We are now awakening to the fact that a product's design is the primary driver of all major life cycle value and waste. Some 70 to 80 percent of all value and waste is created by poor design solutions.

For many organizations with mature lean manufacturing and six sigma initiatives, most of the low-hanging factory floor fruit has already been plucked.

Now the opportunity is to turn to the product development phase to make products even *leaner by design.*

The lean revolution is migrating upstream to the product development arena.

Integrated Lean Design Model

The *Lean Design Solution* process helps you integrate the entire body of lean design knowledge.

I have acquired this knowledge during my 22 years of experience as a "hands on" product team coach as well as from the research of the best academics and practitioners in the design field.

In writing this book, I have drawn on the best lessons of lean manufacturing design, six sigma analysis, Design for X, Quality Function Deployment and many other successful design methodologies.

The *Lean Design Solution* process you will learn here helps you leverage the use of these tools in an orderly, coherent manner. It gives you a framework for making them even more powerful.

However, *The Lean Design Solution* is not a rehash of existing design technologies.

You will acquire *new* knowledge, never published before, about how to develop a better product.

You will also learn a logical, proven method for assuring that your product team is harnessing the full horsepower of lean design.

Who Will Benefit from This Book

The Lean Design Solution is for those leaders and project team members who have the task of delivering better products faster.

For the sake of brevity, I will be calling all of you *Lean Design Champions.*

Much has been written about the need for "leaner product designs." Little has been written about the "*how to*" of making lean design really work.

This book corrects that by giving you ways to make lean product concepts quickly "*actionable.*"

This is a rubber-hits-the-road book that gives you lean product ideas you can immediately use.

Those who will benefit from this book include:

- **Process improvement leaders** challenged with improving their company's product development process.

- **Lean manufacturing champions** who now have the task of taking the lean revolution "upstream."
- **Six Sigma Black Belts** who want to know how to play a productive role at the product design stage
- **Engineering or manufacturing managers** searching for a way to unify and align their plethora of design tools, techniques and software into a coherent Lean Product Design approach
- **Product design team leaders** looking for a step-by-step way to get their teams focused, on track, and motivated on Day One and beyond.
- **Design team members** looking for techniques to make their new product truly "*lean from the start.*"
- **Senior executives** wanting assurance that lean design decisions are being made in alignment with overall enterprise strategy.

Hands-On Book

This is a "*hands on*" book. You will not read fuzzy abstractions here. What you will get are easy-to-understand, common sense techniques and tools to quickly improve a product for your supply chain, factory floor and customer.

The *Lean Design Solution* helps you answer the tough questions about lean product and process design.

Those who have the job of implementing a lean product development process will find ways to make that task go smoothly and with solid results.

Six Sigma Black Belts and other quality facilitators will especially find this book useful. The tools are easily learned and can be taught quickly. You will find hints, tips and advice for you throughout the book.

If you are a product design team member or leader, you will learn new lean product design techniques, as well as be able to review old ones.

Design Now Everybody's Job

This book is especially good for those on a product team who have little or no design training or experience. This is common today as many different disciplines are now serving on *integrated product design* teams.

All team participants are being asked to play a role in shaping a product design.

Yet few have learned the art and science of "design" in school. And many have little, or very poor, on-the-job training.

So many end up on a product development team with less than perfect design skills and, in many cases, not even knowing what their exact rule is.

Design skills and business skills are converging.

My observation is that folks from marketing, manufacturing, field service and other non-design engineering functions quickly lose interest when they do not know how to contribute proactively at the early concept stage.

The *Lean Design Solution* method corrects that problem. It gives common sense ways to have all "stakeholders" play a meaningful role from concept to design conclusion.

One Product a Year or a Million a Month

The knowledge you learn here is not just for high volume industries.

What you read here will benefit those designing and delivering products at *any volume*.

Whether you are building space satellites at a rate of one per year or pumping out consumer electronics at millions of units per month, you will be able to benefit from this book.

One-per-year satellite builders have been using *Lean Design Solution* techniques for years. The U.S. Navy is using these ideas to design their next generation aircraft carrier.

The *Lean Design Solution* methodology can be used for any construction projects, from a single skyscraper to a thousand home suburban development.

The range of industries now using the *Lean Design Solution* includes:

- Automotive
- Appliance

- Energy
- Construction
- Computer
- Ship Building
- Electronics
- Furniture
- Health
- and many, many more.

The Dual Benefit This Book Gives You

Many folks confuse "product *development* process" with "product *design* process" and suffer from it.

Your *product development process* is an integrated system of sub-processes such as market intelligence gathering, portfolio planning, phase gate review and others for managing your overall product delivery system. It is a true "mega process."

The primary objective of this overarching mega process is to enhance the rubber-hits-the-road task of creating discrete products. This is your *product design process.*

Most times, authors focus on improving the product development process and give short shrift to the actual design of a product.

If "product design" is covered, it is usually at the back of their book and includes a brief overview of "design tools."

The challenge of how to actually design a product is almost an afterthought.

Not so here. I have written this book to correct that flaw. It will help you design both a *lean product development process* and *leaner product designs.*

It harmonizes *lean product development* improvement with *lean product design* improvement.

An important fact: *Never try to improve one without improving the other at the same time.*

The best product development process in the world is of no value if it does not directly result in good product design.

And the best product design team has little chance of success without the direction, support and leadership of an effective product development process.

The *Lean Design Solution* method is a "paradigm buster." It gives you a fresh, new way to create products with far more value and far less waste. Everything you will read here is *"actionable."*

You will get ideas, tools and techniques you can use immediately.

Strengthens Your Design "Infrastructure"

What you read here will not obsolete any product design tool, technique, or software you now have in place. It will, however, enable you to leverage these in a far more powerful way.

Applying the *Lean Design Solution* will enhance your Six Sigma and lean manufacturing tools.

It will help you focus your *Value Stream Mapping* (VSM) efforts both on the factory floor and in your product development efforts. Your phase gate reviews will be even more beneficial.

You need not "give up" any existing techniques or tools when applying the *Lean Design Solution.*

Stronger Ownership

The *Lean Design Solution* places ownership of the design process squarely in the hands of *all product stakeholders.*

These are the folks who must help deliver the new product . or who will be affected by it once it is in the field.

The *Lean Design Solution* gives stakeholders a voice, a role and a step-by-step method for participating in the design process. Very importantly, it helps the design team leader apply his leadership talents in an effective and efficient manner.

The way the *Lean Design Solution* does this is with the use of its keystone tool, *Lean Design Mapping (LDM).*

This is a team-based, step-by-step way for figuring out the best strategy for developing your new product.

Lean Design Mapping helps you and your team find the right customer values you must embed in your new product.

And it enables you to create a strategy for preventing life cycle product waste with better design solutions.

Lean Design Mapping enables a Black Belt or lean champion with virtually no product design experience to play a valuable role in moving his company forward in the quest for better product development.

You will learn the *"What, Why and How To"* of *LDM* work. This includes tools, techniques and templates for coaching product design teams.

At the end of each chapter are tools you can use immediately. All are proven ways to roll out lean design quickly.

Easy to Read

I have written this book in an easy-to-read manner. Everyone on your team will be able to both understand and apply what is in this book.

This is true whether you are from marketing, manufacturing, engineering, purchasing or any other function.

My 22 years of experience as a product design coach have taught me that we learn best from concrete examples and highly visual descriptions. That's why this book is filled with stories and anecdotes, not difficult-to-understand abstractions.

You will learn about the Swedish ship *VASA* that sunk two hours into its maiden voyage in 1628 due to a severe lack of "lean thinking."

You will hear about how the Battle of Britain was almost lost due to the *Gremlins of Waste* infesting the famous Spitfire.

You will learn how Ray Kroc, founder of McDonalds, Sam Walton, the man who gave us Wal-Mart, and Bill Gates of Microsoft all applied the same equation to become billionaires.

You will discover the secret of that equation, now known as the *Universal Lean Product Equation*, and how you can apply it to get similar results.

Design of This Book

I have designed this book with six chapters. Each gives you a major element you need to create a truly lean product design.

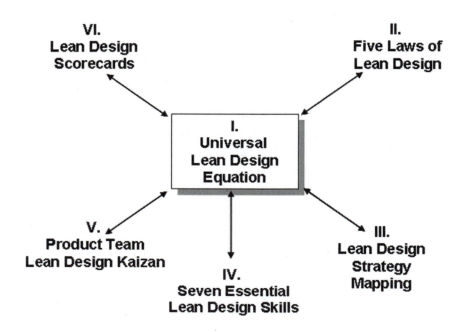

Chapter 1 - The Universal Lean Design Equation. Lean products start with solving the right equation. Here you will learn the *Universal Lean Product Equation.* This at the heart of the *Lean Design Solution.* Knowing this equation is the first step in you quest for a lean product design.

Chapter 2 - The Five Laws of Lean Design. In this chapter I will share with you the *Five Laws of Lean Design* that govern how well you are able to solve the *Universal Lean Product Equation.*

- *Law of Strategic Value.* How to find the values your customer really seeks.
- *Law of Waste Prevention.* How to prevent waste creation right at the start.
- *Law of Marketplace Pull.* How to recognize new opportunities long before your competitor does.
- *Law of Innovation Flow.* How to create a stream of successful products.
- *Law of Fast Feedback.* How to know if you are on the right road to success.

Chapter 3 - Lean Product Strategy Thinking. Here I will introduce you to a powerful tool for getting your product team strategically headed in the right direction. This technique, *Lean Design Mapping (LDM)*, is the "keystone tool" of the *Lean Design Solution.*

Chapter 4 - Seven Essential Design Skills. In this chapter I will describe the seven top skills every team member needs to know. These are useful for any kind of product or service. You need not have any deep technical experience to understand and apply these skills.

Chapter 5 - Product Team Design Kaizan. A good beginning for your design effort is the key to a good ending. Here you will learn how to conduct an intensive, step-by-step workshop for applying the *Lean Design Mapping* to create your product strategy.

Chapter 6 - Product Design Scorecards. You won't know if you have a winning design unless you keep score. In this chapter you will learn how to create *Lean Design Scorecards.* These are tools for comparing alternative designs to reach the right product decision.

What This Book Is Not

This is not a book on "team building." I strongly believe in the need for team building skills, but product teams today mainly fail because of *poor design skills.*

This book will show you how to *sharpen your design skills* so that you can be far more effective and efficient as a product team.

This book is also not just a collection of Japanese design techniques. I understand all these techniques and find them effective when applied at the right time, in the right way and by the right people.

But the most effective product design tools are those developed for the culture in which they will be used. This book is filled with design tools *"made in America"* for our uniquely creative environment.

They may not be used by Toyota and other well-known Japanese companies; however, they will deliver the same results.

And this book is not another "design for manufacturability" book. I was a leader of the "design for manufacture and assembly" (DFMA) movement and wholeheartedly support any effort to reduce factory costs.

But many times the greatest competitive advantage is not to be gained from "manufacturability." In fact, you can design for manufacturability yet seriously degrade the overall success of your product.

This is a book that shows you how to design for all the "*Ilities*", ones such as marketability, installability, maintainability, and all those you need to integrate into your design to make it successful.

Finally, this is not a book about Toyota lean product development methods. Much has been written about Toyota's capability to design world class products.

I will, however, be describing many Toyota techniques as recounted by the excellent studies done in the past few years.

You will read about American companies who have applied "lean thinking" long before Toyota's "lean manufacturing" became known to the western world.

What this book will do is show you how to achieve the same results Toyota does by using common sense "made in America" tools.

Who I Am and What I Do

What you will read here is what I have learned over the past 22 years. That is how long I have been training and coaching product design teams, as well as helping companies to improve their product development processes.

Let me first say that the techniques, tools and methods you will learn here did not originate in the hallowed halls of academia.

I have a good deal of respect for the dozens of university professors who have penned books on product development. I have read most of them.

However, I have found the most profound knowledge about good product design comes from the people in the field who must do it every day.

That means *you*.

What you will learn here comes from the collective experience of thousands of product teams around the world. I have logged millions of miles working with and, most importantly, learning from these teams.

Collective Experience of Many Product Teams

Over the years, I learned the secrets of why some product design teams fail and others win. I found that winning teams, many times unwittingly, solved their product development problems in a unique, yet consistent manner.

My long experience with Japanese companies, gained while I was partnering with them as owner of my own automated assembly machine tool business, also gave me valuable insights.

I began to construct a design method based on what I learned.

I trained many teams in this method, observing the results and then improving the tools and techniques further. The *Lean Design Solution* you will read about here is based on what I learned from working with these teams.

So the real "author" of this book is not me. It's the thousands of product teams I have had the good fortune of knowing over the past two decades.

Pure theory does not abound here. Solid, common sense experience does.

More Than *One Thousand* Companies

This book is based on the collective experience of working with more than one thousand companies.

I have devoted most of my adult life to working with design teams.

Most of my career has been as a "team coach" for those wanting to reshape their product development process or wanting to deliver better product designs.

Most of my work is done "on-site," where the design action really happens. My frequent flyer accounts are overflowing. I have probably worked with more product teams than any person alive today.

For many years, I have resisted writing this book. My livelihood has come from giving on-site training, coaching, and consulting in the technology of product design and development.

This is the first time the *Lean Product Solution* method has been published.

Many times my clients requested that their successes with the *Lean Design Solution* not be published. They rightly viewed the techniques they learned as giving them a distinct competitive edge.

Companies Now Harvesting Benefits

Today, however, more than 200,000 have been trained in the techniques of *Lean Design Solution* and are harvesting its benefits.

No longer is it considered a "secret."

What you will read here is what I have learned from hard working folks in the thick of the real product design action. I owe everything I know to them.

They are the real authors of this book.

Should you be one of the thousands I have had the pleasure of working with, some of what you read here may be familiar, albeit with some new twists. Indeed, you may have even helped shape some of these concepts.

To you I especially say thanks. I am in your debt.

If you are new to lean product design, my goal is to have you immediately benefit from the collective experience I have gained from these thousands of lean product design champions.

So this book is based not on my theories, but on their common sense.

I hope you enjoy this book as much as I have enjoyed learning this common sense though all these years.

Bart Huthwaite, Sr.
Founder
Institute for Lean Design
www.LeanDesign.org
Mackinac Island, Michigan
Spring, 2004

Introduction

It's Monday morning and your boss wants some answers.

More than a month ago he asked you to head up your company's new *Lean Design Initiative.*

"We need a way to get leaner product designs," he confided as he walked you to his office door, arm around your shoulder.

"And we need a good way to do it quickly!" he emphasized.

You already know your company's lean manufacturing transformation has been underway successfully for several years.

Your company has had outstanding success on the factory floor.

But now the lean revolution is starting to wash upon your product engineering shores. And you've been given the job of making it work in the product design arena.

You remember George. This was the fellow who was given the task of introducing your company's "Phase Gate Review" process several years back.

> Lean design is the power to do less of what doesn't matter and more of what does matter.

George is still recovering from that traumatic experience.

It's now been a month since that fateful talk and your boss is itching for an answer. And you are still struggling with the step-by-step *how to* of launching your assignment.

It's not that you haven't tried.

You've benchmarked other companies. You have studied articles in MIT's *Sloan Management Review* and the *Harvard Business Review*.

You even attended a *Lean by Design* Conference.

You also have a growing stack of books scattered about your office.

Lean Design "Smoke and Mirrors"

You even searched out studies on how Toyota, the "birthplace" of lean manufacturing, does product development. But everything you read about Toyota's approach seems like a lot of "smoke and mirrors."

Many of the folks in your company are trained in Value Stream Mapping, Design for Six Sigma, QFD, Design for Manufacturing and Assembly, and Taguchi Methods.

But these are "tools," not an *integrated* lean product design process.

You have yet to satisfy yourself that you have found the rubber-hits-the-road way forward that your boss is patiently awaiting.

Most of what you have learned is the *what* of lean product design and very little about the *how to*.

What you need is practical guidance in making lean design really happen at the product team level.

And you don't want to have to throw away any of the tools you already have in use.

Sound familiar? Don't feel alone. Join the crowd.

Almost all of the lean design champions I meet are frustrated by the lack of a step-by-step solution for creating a truly lean product design.

I wrote this book, the *Lean Design Solution*, to solve that dilemma.

What Does "Lean Product Design" Really Mean?

In my daily work with lean champions, I sometimes find confusion about the words *"lean product design."* Many are frustrated by how to explain lean design in a clear, persuasive way.

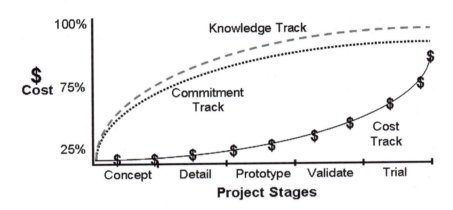

Lean Product Design means two things. These powerful three words can be used as both a *verb* and a *noun*.

A *lean product design* is one that has been created to deliver high value with low waste. Used in this sense it is a *noun*.

Those words are also used to describe the *design process* used to create such a product. In this case the words are used as an active *verb*.

In either case, the primary message is that both the *process* and the *product* must deliver far greater value with less waste than conventional product efforts.

A key point is that lean design is far more than just eliminating factory floor *waste*. It is eliminating waste for your customer and suppliers as well.

And very importantly, it's all about *creating value* for both your customer and company alike.

How you design your product will drive 70 to 80 percent of its eventual success.

Using the *Lean Design Solution* method will give you the knowledge you need to be on track right from the start.

A Closer Look at "Lean Product Design"

By **lean** I mean a product or a product development process that delivers value with less waste. "Value" means benefits for the customer, your company, your supply chain and any other stakeholders who are affected by the creation or use of the product.

What I *don't* mean is just *lean manufacturing value.* A lean product must deliver value well beyond your factory floor.

Case in Point: Toyota's product design process is not just famous for delivering "manufacturability."

It is best known today for delivering value to customers who are constantly seeking better deliverability, serviceability, style, and other differentiators of value in the automotive world.

Toyota is constantly working on reducing waste for the customer. Its new models are designed to constantly lower wasteful serviceability costs in both time and money.

By **product** I mean the sum of all the elements a product requires over the span of its lifecycle. This includes a product's functions, parts, *lifecycle* processes, material, and human labor.

I will use the word "product" in this book to refer to not only the physical parts of the product, but all the tasks required to design, manufacture, sell, service and dispose of it.

By **lifecycle** I mean a product's existence from "lust to dust," or from creation to disposal. I originally used the words "cradle to the grave" to describe what I meant by lifecycle.

This was until a product team member corrected me.

He pointed out that some of the most disastrous mistakes are made in the "product lust" phase. And some of the most expensive costs occur in the "disposal" phase.

Example: The disposal phase of a product is gathering a lot of attention. Take for example, Shaw Industries Inc., the world's largest carpet maker. Shaw is now delivering *re-usability* with a major product line.

The carpeting is fully recyclable. Most traditional carpet usually ends up in a landfill.

Architect William McDonough and German chemist Michael Braungart developed such an approach with their design idea called "cradle-to-cradle." (See their book *Cradle to Cradle: Remaking the Way We Make Things* [North Point Press].)

Shaw's new carpet line now uses materials that are fully reusable as new carpet fiber. Re-usability is saving Shaw money. Their new product has already cut manufacturing costs by 10 percent.

Herman Miller, Inc., a leading office chair manufacturer, has also taken up the cause of "cradle-to-cradle." It is now offering a new chair with materials that can be disassembled and 96 percent of them reused and recycled.

By *design* I mean the tasks done and actions taken to develop the physical product. I also mean the organizational processes used to support that physical design effort.

This now means the involvement of virtually every department in a company. Product design is now everybody's job.

Case in Point: The magazine *Fast Company* points out the importance of design being everybody's job in an article entitled, "Masters of Design: 20 Creative Mavericks and What You Can Learn From Them."

"If you are mapping out a sale strategy, or streamlining a manufacturing operation, or crafting a new system for innovating—if you work in the real world of business—you are engaged in the practice of design."

The Roots of Lean Product Design

The word "lean" has its roots in the lean manufacturing revolution that is now well along in sweeping the industrialized world.

The word "lean" itself was coined by a researcher, John Krafcik, working on the MIT team that eventually gave the world the classic book, *The Machine That Changed the World.*

That book introduced the Toyota continuous-flow production method that reduces direct labor, virtually eliminates work-in-process and component inventory, and improves quality.

Krafcik used "lean manufacturing" to describe what is now known as the Toyota Production Method. At the time, it was a way quite contrary to how automobiles were being mass produced in the West.

The Machine That Changed the World signaled the beginning of the end of *mass production* for many high volume industries.

Lean manufacturing means less of everything, from inventory to labor to machines. The core idea in lean manufacturing is to strip away all "wasted effort" leaving only what is of value in the production process.

Today there is scarcely a company in business who doesn't either know about or is already energetically using some kind of lean manufacturing.

Product Design the Real Culprit?

It wasn't long, however, before companies began to discover that factory floor solutions could do only so much. Most product cost is determined by the quality of its design solutions.

Those companies with mature lean manufacturing initiatives soon found that most of the low-hanging fruit had already been harvested with lean manufacturing techniques.

New opportunities would require changing a product's design

However, changing a design once it hits the manufacturing arena is tough sledding. It is costly and very disruptive.

It can create delays that can even result in the loss of the new business actually being sought.

So the "lean revolution" is now expanding upstream to the product design phase.

We are now being asked to design a product *lean from the start.*

And we now realize that "design" is the primary ingredient for a product's true success. We have been spending too much time, too late, and working in the wrong place on "fixing" our product quality, cost and value problems.

The Second Toyota Wake Up Call

A second wake-up call came in the mid-nineties with a new series of revelations about why Toyota is so successful. Dr. Allen Ward, while a professor at the University of Michigan, led a study of Toyota's product development practices.

Sponsored by the National Center for Manufacturing Sciences (NCMS) of Ann Arbor, Michigan, that study found Toyota's success is due just as much to the way it develops products as it is to its famous lean manufacturing methods.

Toyota's design practices were yielding astounding results with almost no reliance on the tools and techniques in vogue in the Western world.

For example, Ward found that Toyota has no formal Six Sigma design process, does no Value Stream Mapping, doesn't co-locate teams and has no standard "phase gate" development process. And there is no reliance on QFD, FMEA, or DFM.

Toyota was, however, consistently the most profitable carmaker, never missed major milestones, developed products 50 percent faster than its competitors and had the highest quality in the automobile industry.

So the scramble was on to find how to duplicate Toyota's product design practices, just as the West had copied Toyota's production methods.

It's now been a decade since Allen Ward's findings. While companies clearly understand *what* Toyota is accomplishing they continue to struggle with the *how to* of accomplishing the same results.

In this book, I will recount some of what researchers have found out about Toyota's product development process. At the same time, I will also share with you the "how to" of achieving the same results here in the Western world.

Lean Manufacturing Tools Difficult at Design Stage

Most lean manufacturing tools cannot be directly applied to the product design arena.

Why? Factory floor processes and product design processes are two different animals. Manufacturing processes are serial and highly visible.

The waste within factory floor processes can be systematically identified with techniques such as *Value Stream Mapping (VSM)*.

However, product design processes are not serial, not visible and the worst waste appears well downstream in factory, or worse, when the product reaches the customer.

Factory floor lean manufacturing techniques require *analytical skills* to eliminate waste. Attacking waste by design requires *preventive skills*, eliminating the waste before it even reaches the shop floor.

Savings from lean manufacturing efforts can be measured relatively easily. This is far from the case with the *forecasted savings* from lean product design.

While cost reductions in direct material and direct labor can be predicted, reductions in indirect "overhead" costs are almost impossible to estimate with any accuracy.

Savings in customer indirect costs are even more challenging to forecast.

The Toyota Experience

The Toyota Production Method was virtually imported "whole" from Japan. It came complete with a Japanese lexicon that is still being used today.

In sharp contrast, adopting Toyota's product development process has been a frustrating challenge. It has none of the "step-by-step" of the Toyota Production System.

Even deep studies into Toyota's product development practices led nowhere for those seeking the "secrets" of its success.

A lot of this fog is clearing today as Toyota observers characterize what Toyota does as "knowledge-based product development." (For an excellent account of this, read Michael N. Kennedy's *Product Development for the Lean Enterprise: Why Toyota's System is Four Times More Productive and How You Can Implement It.)*

Observers have found Toyota's six strong product design points to be:

1. Deep understanding of the values customers seek
2. Close supplier integration in the design process
3. Strong technical and entrepreneurial project leadership
4. Retention of knowledge for easy retrieval and re-use
5. Strong knowledge sharing and convergence between stakeholders
6. High workforce skills and sense of responsibility

Read this list a second time and you will find Toyota's strategy to be based on good old common sense. These are goals any sensible company seeks.

"How To" Solution Missing

What has been missing in this quest for duplicating Toyota's results is the "how to." Many commentators are strong on the "what and why" of lean product design but very short on this "how to."

This *Lean Design Solution* corrects that problem by giving easily digestible, easy to apply techniques and tools. Reading this book will give you "made in America" ways for accomplishing all six of Toyota's strong points noted above.

I am not saying the approach you read here is the *only* way to achieve these goals. There are many roads to Rome.

However, I am saying that if you apply the concepts and tools of the *Lean Design Solution* you will be well on your way to beating Toyota at its own game.

Universal Lean Design Equation

From my work with hundreds of design teams, I have discovered that all lean products are the result of solving a simple, yet elegant, equation.

This equation is universal. It applies to products, services and processes.

Once you use it, you will never forget it.

I call it the *Universal Lean Product Equation.* It has never been challenged in all my work with thousands of design teams around the world.

Some design teams solve this equation intuitively. However, most product teams must initially be coached in the "how to" of solving it.

The purpose of this book is to show you how to harness the power of this *Universal Lean Product Equation,* as well as how you can coach others in the use of it.

It is important to understand that this equation did not spring out of my brain one clear day. It emerged from working with people like you who are challenged to help product teams develop better products.

The most successful product teams were those that thought on a higher plane than most. They focused on delivering "product values," not just product requirements.

They typically referred to these values as *"Ilities,"* as in *manufacturability.*

Process Thinking Needed

They were also strong "process thinkers." They saw that a product was the lifecycle sum of all the actions or tasks required to deliver that value.

They understood that every task, action or "process" took time, hence cost money, and if required and not done well, could create a quality flaw.

Simply reducing the number and complexity of the process steps could lead to both costs savings and quality improvement.

I began expressing this equation in a few simple words. I used these words to begin all my workshops:

Optimize Product Values, Prevent Wasteful Processes

"Product values" means all those product characteristics customers desire. These are attributes such as *affordability, usability, reliability, maintainability* and many others.

However *values* are a two-way street. They also mean those benefits your company desires from the product.

These are such things as *profitability, manufacturability, riskability, marketability* and many more.

It is important to remember that value creation must be a two-headed coin, delivering benefit to both your customer and your company.

Prevent Wasteful Processes

"Wasteful processes" are those activities along a product's *total life cycle* that do not create value. These are such things as *stocking, storing, repairing,* or what are now known as unneeded *"Ings."*

Lean manufacturing champions call these wasteful tasks *muda,* the Japanese word for *waste.*

Wasteful *muda* on your factory floor and in your supply chain is such tasks as *inventorying, storing, checking, re-working*, and many others.

However, many times the greatest opportunity for waste elimination is *not* within your manufacturing process.

The best targets may be the waste your customers suffer from *learning, installing, using, servicing* and finally *disposing* of your product.

I call this kind of customer waste *"super muda."*

Unfortunately, from time-to-time I encounter companies focusing their entire lean design improvement effort solely on reducing manufactured cost.

Ignoring the potential for creating customer *super muda* can be disastrous. You may end up improving manufacturing cost but severely compromise customer values such as maintainability.

For example, optimizing manufacturability without paying close attention to serviceability can result in the classic case of having to remove your car's right front wheel to change the oil.

Focusing Your Lean Design Equation

This equation worked well; however, design teams soon began to challenge me as to *what kind of values?* and *what kind of wasteful processes?*

The hallmark of all good design efforts is iteration.

So I began to take a lesson from my own coaching tip: *Your first design is never the best; the last is only a step in the right direction.*

I began to iterate this equation to make it more *understandable* and *actionable* for lean design champions as well as "hands on" design teams.

I shared with them what I had learned from experience are the *Eight Primary Values* all customers want. I also shared with them the *Eight Primary Values* their own company desires.

Since the early days of *Lean Product Design*, I had always been searching for a way to communicate what lean product thinking was all about. It was a frustrating experience.

Expressing this equation in a few simple words continued to elude me.

My definitions always seemed to get more complicated, rather than simpler. This was in clear violation of my constant admonitions about simplifying everything.

The major breakthrough came one evening over coffee. I had just finished having dinner with a friend of mine, the engineering vice-president of a major client.

Put *Ility* Values In and Take Wasteful *Ings* Out

That day I had talked about the importance of putting *Ility* values in and taking wasteful *Ings* out of his company's products. And I had shared with his fellow managers the evils that could arise from not preventing these from ever happening with better design.

Then I remembered what a wise friend once told me:

If you can't clearly express a concept on the back of a business card, you really can't communicate it well.

So like any good Tom Sawyer, I challenged my client to write his description of my lean design equation on the back of his business card.

He hardly paused a moment. Quickly reaching into his pocket for a pen and his card, he scrawled the following words:

Optimize Strategic Ilities, Minimize Evil Ings!

I was stunned. My friend had captured in a few words what took me hours to communicate.

To this day, I have never had anyone effectively challenge this six word equation as being the key to product success.

This book will reveal the secrets of how to deliver *Strategic Ilities* to benefit *both* your customer and your company. These secrets will also benefit your suppliers.

It will show you how to identify and minimize the *Evil Ings* that bedevil every product along its lifecycle.

In short, it will show you in a very step-by-step manner the way to solve the *Universal Lean Design Equation.*

Strategic *Ilities* as Key Values

Strategic Ilities are those primary product values, or attributes, that both your customer and company seek from a product.

A product must deliver dozens of *Ilities.*

However, only a few are really *strategic.* These are the six to eight that are absolutely essential for the product's success. One of the first tasks of a design team is to seek out and focus these strategic values.

All new product efforts must start with a strategy. This strategy must be crafted to benefit all stakeholders in the product's success.

Too many design teams fail to do this. They take a set of "requirements" and rush to the task of solving them.

In Chapter I you will learn the primary values your customers as well as your company seek. You will be able to use these to help craft the right product design strategy.

The word *optimize* means that you will never be able to deliver all values 100 percent. The design process is one of constant trade-offs in order to find the most optimum solution.

Evil Ings Are Wasteful Processes

The words *Evil Ings* mean those processes or tasks that are wasteful throughout your product's life cycle. These wasteful process steps number in the hundreds of thousands for even the least complicated products.

Your task as a lean design champion is to *prevent* these from ever happening.

Creating "maps" of these end-to-end processes by using such techniques as Value Stream Mapping (VSM), would require miles of wall space and a lot of imagination. They are also not highly visible at the design concept stage.

Then there is the problem of doing many maps for many design solutions in order to look at trade-offs. The task quickly becomes mind-boggling.

Fortunately, you don't need to do this. Such an effort would only be attacking the *effect* of bad design. What you must do is attack the *design root causes* of all this waste.

You must use *waste prevention*.

Seven Major Creators of Waste

There are seven major "design drivers" of all product life cycle waste. Knowing these and reducing their impact through smarter design is the key to waste prevention.

In this book you will see me referring to these seven as the *Seven Evil Ings*. Both these *Evil Ings* and the *Strategic Ilities* are predictable. They are measurable. And they are the key to designing leaner products.

This *Optimize Strategic Ilities, Minimize Evil Ings* equation is at the center of the *Lean Design Solution*.

Lean Product Design Not New

In reality, lean product design is not really new.

Only the word "lean" is new.

It has been around since the industrial revolution. Henry Ford was a great practitioner with his design and production of the famous Model T.

Most companies are practicing parts of lean design today. Design for Manufacture and Assembly is one aspect of lean design. It attacks wasteful assembly steps.

Design for Reliability is alive and well with such tools as Failure Modes Effects Analysis (FMEA). And Design for Six Sigma quality (DFSS) is growing stronger every day.

> My constant effort is in the direction of simplicity. Complexity is the enemy. Nearly everything we make is much more complex than it needs to be.
>
> — Henry Ford, an early lean engineer

A Slice Through the Center of the Product Apple

What is lacking, however, is an integrated design approach that simultaneously considers *all of these values* as part of the design equation.

At the same time, this design method must also help a product team eliminate waste, not increase it, with the integration of these values.

As one product team leader once said, "We need a design approach that cuts through the very center of the product apple to the very core. We don't want to take a look at one slice like design for manufacturability or then another sliver for design for reliability. We need the full view."

The *Lean Design Solution* does precisely that. It cuts to the core of the apple.

It is easily learned and easily used by the technically minded and the non-technically minded alike.

None of what you read here will argue with any worthwhile design processes you are now using. It will only enhance them.

In fact, one of the *Lean Design Solution's* biggest benefits is to integrate existing practices with newer lean ideas to create a powerful system of *total lean design thought and action.*

My Personal Journey To Lean Design Thinking

My journey to lean design thinking began more than 20 years ago. Back then I believed *Design for Assembly (DFA)* was the ultimate in good design thinking.

The idea was to reduce wasteful assembly time on the factory floor.

The most popular DFA tactic at that time was part count reduction. Fewer parts meant less assembly time.

Functional integration was the design technique used. You simply tried to integrate the functions of several parts into one part. This was done through the use of engineered plastics, stamping techniques, or similar means.

Not only were you eliminating assembly time, you were also reducing material and manufacturing costs.

And by designing the remaining parts better, you could make manual assembly easier or even automate the parts.

Or so I thought.

I soon found that approach worked well for automotive companies who had high assembly costs. But it didn't work so well for those companies where assembly was not a big deal.

A Personal Lesson in Lean Design

A basic rule of the *Lean Design Solution* is that you must focus on the "strategic," or most important values, or *Ilities*, your customers and company seeks.

An *Ility* value that is important to one customer may be of no consequence to another.

I learned that lesson the hard way.

Some 22 years ago, I sold my automated machine tool company to Nitto Seiko, my Japanese partner. Nitto Seiko is one of Japan's largest automated assembly machine builders.

Nitto Seiko wanted to get into the booming American market for automation. I wanted to move on to more fertile fields and away from the highly cyclical machine tool business.

Nitto Seiko and I struck a deal. I sold my business to them and started my search for a new way to make a living.

I found my new business right under my nose.

Design for Assembly

When I owned my automated assembly machine business, we held customer workshops in how to design products to make them easier to automate.

Many times companies would show up at our door with their bag of parts and a purchase order asking us to build a machine to automate the assembly of their product.

We would do a quick review of their parts. Many did not even lend themselves to automation. They were not designed for automation in the first place.

So we conducted workshops to help their engineers learn the basics of automated assembly parts design, as well as get us in on the ground floor of their new projects.

I called these workshops *Design for Assembly*, or *DFA*.

It wasn't long before Ford Motor heard about these workshops and asked me to train their engineers in DFA skills. The timing was perfect. I had found my new business.

What followed was a rush of Design for Assembly workshops at Ford and their suppliers.

The results were astounding. Product teams could show part counts dropping by 50 to 60 percent. Assembly costs were slashed.

Confirmed Part Thinker

A favorite technique was to convert fasteners (*they are parts!*) into snap fits. Multiple parts were integrated into one part with the use of new engineered plastics.

On paper, factory floor direct costs (assembly labor and materials) plummeted.

Oh, from time-to-time I would hear a few folks say that integrating parts created complexity. They would say that costs such as tooling, testing, and engineering time were going up astronomically.

But we brushed off both those expenses as not being measurable as well as being insignificant.

We were on a "direct cost" money saving binge. I was a confirmed "partist," one who believed that "*fewer parts are always better.*"

Not known then was that many of those DFA part count "successes" would come back to haunt automotive companies years later as serviceability nightmares.

But Ford Motor was on a roll.

Design for Assembly was the path to product excellence! It was so measurable. It was so visible. And it was so easy.

Little did I know that ahead of me were some hard lessons in my journey from a "part thinker" to a "lean product design thinker."

"You Don't Know Our Business!"

It was in Phoenix, Arizona when my "partist" paradigm began to crack. After hearing about my automotive industry success, a jet engine manufacturer invited me out to give a presentation to their senior management.

During my energetic pitch about the benefits of part count reduction, I was interrupted by the manufacturing vice-president who abruptly stood up and said:

"*You don't know our business! And until you do we don't need you here!*"

"*We build jet engines with heat and pressure requirements far tougher than those of the automotive industry,*" he went on, with me getting redder in the face with every passing moment.

"*Reducing parts is not so easy in our business.* "*And our main problem is not assembly cost. It's our factory floor overhead costs,*" he ended, sitting down just as abruptly as he got up.

All of this was very embarrassing.

But he was absolutely right, both with regard to me not knowing his business and his company's opportunity to reduce parts.

After I swiftly ended my talk, I got with the manufacturing vice-president and asked if I could spend time on his factory floor to learn his business better.

That meeting was a turning point in my career as a product design coach.

Process Complexity the Culprit

What I soon learned was that his problem was not parts but *manufacturing processes*. And his assembly process proved to be a relatively minor one.

I discovered that three process "families" were creating most of his cost and quality problems.

These manufacturing processes were:

Complex Manufacturing Processes

These complex processes were created by design solutions requiring multiple machining steps. This meant a lot of handling between machining cells.

Some of these design solutions also required machining on multiple surfaces, which in turn required multiple set ups.

My thinking began to shift from *parts complexity* to *process complexity* as the root cause of the jet engine manufacturer's dilemma. Good lean design is to machine on as few surfaces as possible.

Then I found a second process problem that was making their factory floor problems even worse.

The jet engine design staff was specifying precision when minimum, or even no precision, was necessary.

Precision Manufacturing Processes

Parts were being machined to tolerances well beyond those needed in actual use. It was if the design engineers considered precision to be a positive benefit, no matter whether it was required or not.

Their use of excessive precision was driving the need for more precision tooling, precision machines, and highly skilled operators.

Scrap rates were high due to the difficulty of maintaining the sometimes unneeded precision.

Precision processing is very expensive both to do on the factory floor as well as to maintain in the field.

A breakdown of precision when needed can lead to serious quality problems. The best cure is to avoid precision when it is not absolutely required.

And then I discovered yet another family of processes that was creating havoc on the manufacturing floor.

These were processes that gave *highly variable* results.

Variable Manufacturing Processes

The jet manufacturer's floor was awash in statistical process control (SPC) in an effort to control variable processes such as manual welding and brazing.

All human *Ings,* or process steps, are variable and require a lot of wasteful steps such *documenting, checking, inspecting,* and *correcting.*

The paper trail to validate that all these steps were done was staggering.

Wasteful Indirect Cost

These three types of manufacturing processes, *complexity, precision* and *variability*, were not just creating a lot of wasteful *direct labor* cost. They were also creating unneeded *overhead or indirect* cost, such as inspection, scrap, and repair.

That factory floor experience resulted in what I came call my new design method, *Design for Manufacture and Assembly.*

I quickly developed design techniques to reduce manufacturing complexity, precision and variability. I developed guidelines and "rules" for reducing these three process families.

That Arizona jet engine manufacturer soon simplified its product designs and saved millions in manufacturing processing cost.

The upshot was that I became absolutely convinced I had made the right course corrections.

I was convinced I had the right design equation this time!

That is, until I traveled even further west to Downy, California and the home of the Space Shuttle orbiter.

Space Shuttle Experience

The setting was almost the same as my workshop experience in Arizona.

I was speaking before a group of Space Shuttle engineers and describing my freshly minted *Design for Manufacture and Assembly (DFMA)* method.

This time it was a quiet vice president of engineering in the very back of the room who politely raised his hand. *"Bart,"* he began, *"with all due respect, you don't understand our business."*

I began to feel a cold sweat coming on.

"We don't build jet engines here. And what you are preaching about manufacturability and assembly is not our worst problem."

"Our problem," he continued politely, *"is DIT!"*

That one had me stumped. So I asked, *"What is DIT?"*

"Now I really know you don't understand our business!" he said. *"DIT stands for documentation, inspection and test. These three are huge costs for us!*

"Most of these are impossible to quantify in a bill of material. And many of our guys don't even begin to know how to reduce them in their designs.

"Show us how to reduce DIT with better design and you will have a lot of work here," the vice-president concluded.

Documentation, Inspection and Test as Culprits

Once again, I quickly retreated.

I asked for the opportunity to get to know their business better by spending time on their factory floor.

What I found were the four major process families that drove DIT or "hidden cost." These were in addition to the three families I found at the jet manufacturing plant:

These four new discoveries were:

Sensitive Processes

Sensitive processes were creating a lot of lost time and cost. These were processes that had to be constantly "tweaked" to keep them running.

Process robustness was virtually non-existent. Then there was the cost of keeping these sensitive parts from being damaged. This required a lot of non-value adding steps such as *shielding, protecting,* and *packaging.*

Immature Processes

I discovered there were many techniques being used that were new and untested. The Space Shuttle folks were always looking for a better way.

This required a lot of *documenting, inspecting* and *testing* to make sure the new process would really work well.

Dangerous Processes

These processes required the use of toxic chemicals or dangerous operations. Both human beings and the environment had to be protected against these.

These were creating the need for a lot of *training, protecting,* and *inspecting,* all of which are non-value added tasks.

High Skill Processes

These were the processes that required extensive training for a person to be *certified* in order to perform them.

Then this highly skilled work had to be *documented, inspected* and *tested* as all we human beings perform in a variable manner from time to time.

These seven process families cost millions in *direct cost.*

However, their greatest cost was "hidden" indirect, or "overhead", expense. The Space Shuttle folks couldn't even begin to quantify this kind of cost.

And there was another major DIT penalty — time!

Turnaround time for the shuttle was moving from originally being planned as weeks to months.

Space Shuttle Folks Happy

Working with their engineering teams, I developed design techniques to significantly reduce DIT.

I ended up training thousands of engineers at every major aerospace company in America.

A while later, my design method emerged as *Design for Manufacture, Assembly and Hidden Cost or DFMAHC.*

It was at this point that I was beginning to wonder if all those letters would bother aerospace engineers.

But I need not have worried.

Companies in the space business have acronyms that made my *DFMAHC* look like child's play!

I thought I finally had the *"design for"* cat by the tail. But, once again, I was to be proven absolutely wrong.

This time it happened in Newport News, Virginia, home of Newport News Shipbuilding.

Newport News builds the Navy's aircraft carriers, one of the most complex, awe inspiring machines built by man.

More than five thousand people work, eat, and sleep aboard these nuclear powered giants.

They are filled with high explosives and jet fuel. A carrier deck is a highly dangerous place to work.

And, as you can imagine, they are very expensive to build.

A Lesson from the Aircraft Carrier Folks

I was at the Newport News ship yard talking to a group of senior executives and Navy officers about the benefits of reducing shipbuilding cost with my newly expanded *DFMAHC* design methodology.

This time it was a Navy two-star admiral, responsible for the construction and management of the entire 12-ship carrier fleet, who brought me up short with the statement:

"Our problem, Mr. Huthwaite, is not building the carrier!

"Our problem is TOC! And that stands for Total Ownership Cost, what it takes to keep a carrier operational during its life time," the admiral explained without bothering to ask me if I really knew what it meant.

Well, it wasn't long before I was spending a lot of time prowling through aircraft carriers and other Navy ships looking for ways to reduce what we now call *lifecycle cost.*

That admiral has since become a very good friend. And his goal of reducing aircraft carrier operational cost is now well underway.

A Highly Interesting Journey

My journey to the *Lean Design Solution* has been an interesting one. I now have worked in virtually every manufacturing industry in the Western Hemisphere and Europe.

And I have coached product teams designing everything from software to gas turbines and from barbecue grills to lawn sprinklers.

Applying the *Lean Design Solution* does not obsolete any existing product design tool, technique or method. To the contrary, it helps a design team "knit together" existing design team tools.

Escalator Effect

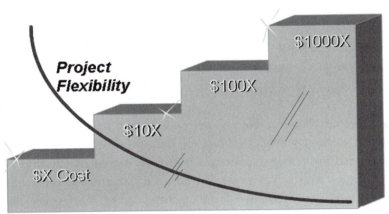

Project Implementation Stages

However, a fundamental of the *Lean Design Solution* is that every new product must start with the *Universal Lean Design Equation* in mind:

Optimize Strategic Ilities, Minimize Evil Ings

How to customize that equation to fit your product design challenge is the subject of the following chapter.

Summary

- "Lean Product Design" refers to both the *process* of creating a product (the verb) as well as the *product* itself (the noun).
- A lean product design is one that *simultaneously* reduces waste and delivers value.
- A product is more than the sum of its parts. It's also the sum of the lifecycle processes needed to design, manufacture and use it.
- The lifecycle of any product is from creation to disposal. In other words, from "lust to dust."

- Product design is now recognized as being "everybody's job." A big challenge is making sure everyone understands their design job description. Using the *Lean Design Solution* solves this problem.
- Most lean manufacturing tools cannot be directly used by a lean design team.
- Lean design savings are hard to predict. Most of the savings will only appear in the sometimes-distant future. Predicting "hidden cost" savings is extremely difficult and questionable given the time it would require.
- Toyota's lean product development process is elusive. It cannot be imported "whole" as was the case with the Toyota Production Method.
- The *Universal Lean Design Equation* is *Optimize Strategic Ilities, Minimize Evil Ings.*
- Strategic *Ilities* are values that will delight your customers as well as differentiate you from your competitors.
- *Evil Ings* are the seven kinds of design solutions that create the most product lifecycle waste.
- The *Lean Design Solution* enables a design team to systematically find the optimum lean design strategy.
- Applying the *Lean Design Solution* does not obsolete any existing product design tool, technique or method. To the contrary, it helps a design team "knit together" existing design team tools.

Chapter 1

The Universal Lean Design Equation
How to Create Value and Reduce Waste

The true measure of a lean design is not just what you take out. It's also what you put in.

In the Introduction, I shared with you the *Universal Lean Design Equation*, sometimes simply called the *Ility and Ing Equation.*

Strategic Ilities are values that will differentiate you from your competitor and deliver delight to your customer.

Evil Ings are wasteful processes created by poor design decisions.

In this chapter, you will learn how to find the *Ility* values that will make your product a winner. I will also share with you how to avoid the *Ings* that bedevil even the best product design efforts.

> Optimize *Strategic Ilities*, Minimize *Evil Ings*

The *Ility and Ing Equation* helps you bring focus to what is truly important for the success of your lean design effort.

This equation can be used with *any* kind of product and at any volume. This is whether you are producing one product a year or a million a month.

The *Ility and Ing Equation* is also valid for everything from software to gas turbine engines.

Understanding it is the first step in applying the *Lean Design Solution.*

Similar to Lean Manufacturing

The *Ility and Ing Equation* is a *customer driven* equation. It operates in a "pull" manner, responding to the wishes of the external marketplace.

This is very similar to how lean manufacturing works on the factory floor.

Products are not "pushed" out the door. Instead, the factory responds to the "pull" of customer demand.

The *Ility and Ing Equation* also says your design must *prevent* the emergence of wasteful tasks (*Ings*) during a product's entire life cycle.

This equation defines a "lean" design as being one that meets both of these requirements at the same time.

It is highly actionable, responsive to customer wishes, and focused on preventing waste before it can occur. This equation harmonizes with the lean manufacturing revolution.

Solving this equation begins with an understanding of the eight *Customer Primary Values*, or *Ilities*, all customers desire.

These primary values are the starting point for your team to craft your own customized product design values, tailored to your specific product or process challenge.

Your Customer's Eight Primary Values

All customers desire eight basic benefits from a product. They may express these values in many different ways, but they underlie every customer's wishes.

For example, all want *performability*, the assurance that the product will function the way they expect. This can be expressed in many ways, such as speed attained, weight lifted and time taken to accomplish a task

Customers also want *affordability*, the knowledge that your product will be within their cost expectations.

You must understand the "voice of the customer" with regard to all of these, as well as listen for the voices of non-customers who are looking for similar values.

However, as I will discuss in the next chapter, your design team must go well beyond just listening to what your customer is saying today. It must *anticipate* what the customer will be seeking in the future.

Each of these *Customer Primary Values* will carry a different weight in your design equation, depending on the nature of the product challenge at hand.

No two design challenges will ever have the same *Ility* values as objectives.

This is because every design challenge is unique unto itself.

Here are the Eight Primary Customer Values:

Primary Customer Values	Customer Questions
Peformability	*Will the product perform as I expect it to?*
Affordability	*Will it be within my cost expectations?*
Featureability	*Will it provide added benefits?*
Deliverability	*Will it be ready for me when I want it?*
Usability	*Can I quickly and easily install it and learn to use it?*
Maintainability	*How easy will it be for me to keep in service?*
Durability	*Is it robust enough to withstand abuse?*
Imageability	*Will it convey an image of quality and prestige?*

The *Lean Design Solution* uses these eight primary values as a checklist to begin the search for the *specific values* that will make your product a success.

For example, *performability* can mean many different things. The task of your lean design team is to define this value as your customer perceives it.

The *Lean Design Solution* helps you do this.

Value as a Two-Headed Coin

While it is crucial that your design is good for the customer, at the same time it must deliver values to your company.

At the same time, your company wants eight *primary benefits* from your new product. For example, *profitability*, is probably at the top of the list. Here again, this can be expressed in many ways.

However, there is also *growability*, the knowledge that your product can lead to ever-increasing sales.

Then there is *investability*, the knowledge that your product makes sense in terms of the time and money needed to bring it to market and keep it there.

The *Lean Design Solution* uses these *Primary Company Values* as a checklist for identifying the specific values that will meet your organization's strategic goals.

Primary Customer Values	Company Management Questions
Profitability	*Will it deliver profits at an acceptable level?*
Investability	*Does this make sense in terms of payback?*
Riskability	*Are the risks we must take prudent?*
Produceability	*Can the factory and supply chain deliver this?*
Marketability	*Do we have the means to sell this?*
Growability	*Does this offer growth and market expansion?*
Leverageability	*Does this build on our core competencies?*
Respectability	*Will this strengthen our reputation?*

Preventing Wasteful *Ings*

The *Lean Design Solution* is based on a *process view* of products and services. This is the thinking that all products are the sum of the processes, or tasks, used to create and deliver that product's values during its entire lifecycle.

To be sure, a product is also the sum of the functions it performs. It is also the sum of the parts that deliver those functions, as well as the material required and the labor needed to perform those values.

But the *fundamental unit* underlying the delivery of all values are *process steps*, or *tasks*. As you well know by now, I call these steps *Ings*.

For example, "parts" are simply the process steps used to create them, locked in a geometric shape. Parts are *things*, or simply combinations of *Ings*.

Process *Ings* are required to deliver the values of all products. Reducing both the number and complexity of these *Ings* is the key to lower cost and, very importantly, better quality.

Each *Ing* takes time to perform, costs money and, if not done in a certain way as required, can cause a quality flaw.

Many product teams unwittingly set wasteful *Ings* in motion by using bad design solutions. One of the major reasons is because our accounting feedback systems do not reveal much about the source of this waste.

Indirect Cost Reduction Hidden from Design Team's View

The most wasteful *Ings* on your factory floor, such as storing, reworking, and transporting, are "hidden" from the design team's view.

In contrast, "visible" *Ings* such as casting, machining, painting and other direct labor and material processes are continually being attacked by design teams because they can be seen, heard, and even smelled.

They are also given better data on these costs.

Your accounting department makes the cost of these *Ings* highly visible through the use of *direct labor and material* reporting. The hidden *Ings* remain hidden in what is called "overhead" or "burden" or "indirect cost."

They are then spread or, as this practice is sometimes called "peanut buttered," over many products as a constant "labor/burden" factor.

The result is that a design team has no *cause and effect* relationship to guide them in reducing these kinds of hidden *Ings*.

A design team has no equation to see the linkage between these hidden *Ing* indirect costs and what they can do to prevent them with better design.

Incredibly, many design teams exclude these hidden costs from their design equation, arguing that since they can't be accurately accounted for, they should not be part of their cost reduction challenge.

The problem of hidden cost is ignored at the design stage and left for factory floor folks to solve.

One of the greatest benefits of the *Lean Design Solution* is that it makes these kinds of hidden costs part of the design equation.

Indirect Product Costs Biggest Challenge

Ignoring a problem only makes it grow.

Overhead costs are the biggest challenge in business today and the most rapidly growing kind of cost. In many companies today, the cost of these *Hidden Ings* is two to three times greater than *Visible Ings.*

The lean manufacturing revolution and techniques such as Value Stream Mapping surfaces these costs so that many can be eliminated.

Yet some cannot be addressed as they are being created by the complexity of the product design.

When I first start training design teams in the *Lean Design Solution,* I always ask how they are reducing indirect cost with smarter design solutions.

Immediately I am given example after example of how they are cutting direct labor and material cost. But only few times am I ever shown how their design is attacking hidden cost.

Product teams are not required or rewarded for reducing *Hidden Ing* cost. They don't have a process to use to even take that kind of action.

Failure to Get at Root of the Problem

So the bottom line is that the overhead problem continues. And like any problem that is not addressed, it just keeps getting bigger.

The *Ility and Ing Equation* gives design teams the means to attack this problem. It makes hidden cost part of the design equation.

I personally welcomed the arrival of lean manufacturing with open arms. For years, I protested against hidden waste creation through bad design decisions.

Most times my protests were met with a shrug and the comment that "it isn't my job."

Lean manufacturing says non-direct labor costs are some of the most expensive on the shop floor. Lean thinking attacks costs in all forms.

Very importantly, those who embraced lean thinking early on did not rely on volumes of "quantitative data" to "prove" the savings that can be achieved.

Product Lifecycle Waste

There are seven types of design solutions that create the most product waste or *Ings*. These seven are also the root cause of most quality problems throughout your product's lifecycle.

By simply minimizing the use of these *Evil Ings*, you will achieve a very significant reduction in cost. You will also get a significant improvement in quality.

Here are the seven:

The Seven Worst Solutions	Description	Wasteful Ings Set in Motion
Complex	Many different processes, high quantity required to deliver the product's value both on factory floor and in the customer's use.	Scheduling, tracking, moving, stocking, handling, etc.
Precise	Solution requiring precision at the outer limits of manufacturer's ability to produce the product or customer's ability to use it.	Training, tooling, inspecting, reworking, learning, misusing, etc.
Variable	Specification of difficult to control processes on the factory floor or in the customer's domain	Certifying, inspecting, reworking, scrapping, etc.
Sensitive	Product easily flawed during factory operations or in the customer's domain	Protecting, packaging, reworking, servicing, etc.
Immature	Use of solutions not previously validated for a specific application	Validating, testing, learning, etc.
Dangerous	Solutions with potential dangerous impact on humans or environment	Monitoring, protecting, documenting, disposing, etc.
Skill Intensive	Solutions requiring relatively high degree of training and experience	Training, certifying, supervising, monitoring, etc.

Using the *Ility and Ing Equation* helps you prevent these worst kinds of *Ings* from ever emerging on your factory floor and throughout your product's lifecycle.

It helps you eliminate waste at its roots without compromising value.

Four Product Domains

Evil Ings can emerge at any time during your product's lifecycle. All products pass through four "domains" during their "lust to dust" lifetime:

- *Design Domain.* All the tasks required to conceptualize, proto-type, test, and detail your product
- *Supply Domain.* All the tasks your suppliers perform in delivering components and services to you
- *Manufacturing Domain.* The tasks needed to convert drawings into components and finally a product
- *User Domain.* All the tasks the customer must do to install, learn, use, maintain and finally dispose of your product.

By far, the *User Domain* continues to offer the greatest opportunity for waste reduction. It also can pay you the greatest rewards in terms of customer satisfaction and new business.

However, the *Design Domain* can result in a lot of costly *Ings*, especially with a new product that uses new technology. Such designing brings with it a lot of testing, validating, documenting, and much more.

Theoretically, the best kind of a design is the one with little or no new design.

Four Domains Offer Lean Opportunity

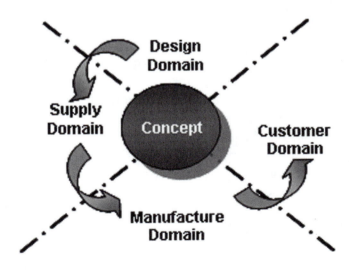

That's why lean design thinkers always first seek previously used solutions or standard off-the-shelf solutions.

Of course, the ideal trick is not to use these kinds of solutions at all. However, we all know that is impossible. So the next best thing is to reduce their *impact* as much as possible.

The worst *Ings* are the ones that rear their heads in your customer's domain. These can be things like excessive learning, installing, maintaining, and thousands of others.

On the factory floor, lean manufacturing practitioners call all waste *muda*. I like to use the term "*super muda*" to describe the kind of *customer* waste created by bad design.

Super muda can kill products and anger customers. Examples are jet engines that require thick manuals to understand how to service them. Or barbeque grills that require two hours to assemble on a hot Saturday afternoon.

Or it can be automobiles that demand that you be a contortionist to change the oil.

The *Ility and Ing Equation* is used to reduce both factory floor *muda* as well as *super muda* in the customer's domain.

The "how to" of doing this is the subject of Chapter Four, 'The Eight Top Lean Design Tactics."

Bring Value and Waste to Life

Lean design is a constant struggle between the forces of value (*Ilities*) and the forces of waste *(Ings)*.

For years I struggled with how to communicate this struggle. Both "value" and "waste" are abstract words.

It was a constant dilemma.

That is, until one of my workshop participants revealed his secret for communicating abstract thoughts over a cold beer one evening. "Cartoons," he said leaning forward to make his point, "Cartoon characters!"

Grabbing a paper napkin he began to sketch his cartoon impersonation of the *Ility* value of *maintainability*, a washing machine repairman dozing with feet up on his desk and cobwebs between his feet and the phone.

Without even pausing a moment, the then sketched his personification of *complexity*, a major villain in creating endless waste. This character turned out to be a multi-armed gremlin with multiple parts and many tools.

"Personify value and waste as characters," he suggested. *"Bring those abstractions to life!"*

What he taught me was that cartoon characters were really exaggerations of ideas, a way of expressing abstractions in a clearer, more powerful manner.

So I took him up on the idea.

I brought the *Eight Primary Customer Values* to life as the *Good Ility Value Brothers.*

Battling them are the *Evil Ing Gremlins.* They are the characters that create most of the waste we see, not only within our own company walls but, much worse, out in the customer's domain.

Designing a lean product is a constant tug of war between these forces of good and evil.

Too often, this struggle goes unseen and unheeded. Evil waste wins out over good value simply because we don't recognize this battle.

You will get a closer look at these characters in the next chapter, "The Five Laws of Lean Design."

Lean design champions find them to be a colorful way to show what lean value and waste is all about.

Lean Design Constant Struggle Between Forces of Good & Evil

Good Ility Value Brothers   Wasteful Ing Gremlins

Product Design is a Tug-of-War between the Forces of Value and Waste

Lean Design Solution as a Six Sigma Quality Tool

We use the term *Ing Busting* to describe the systematic process of identifying and eliminating waste with better design.

Ing Busting will give you far more than just cost reduction. It will help you achieve Six Sigma results. The *Lean Design Solution* is a powerful ally of Six Sigma and other quality improvement initiatives.

The *Lean Design Solution* says that every product is the sum of its *life cycle processes*. Hence, every process step, or *Ing*, takes time and thus costs money.

Most important, though, every process step can trigger a quality problem if done incorrectly.

This is the same belief held by quality experts everywhere. This *Ing* view of the world is nothing new to either Black Belts or lean manufacturing champions.

Black Belts know that one of the most powerful ways to improve quality and achieve Six Sigma results is simply to *reduce the number of process steps* a product requires to either produce it or use it.

Likewise, lean manufacturing champions also live in the world of *Ings*. They are constantly mapping and eliminating non-value added *Ings* in order to reduce waste and improve quality on the production floor.

The worst *Ings* we see on the factory floor are simply the *effects* of poor design. The complexity of a design is the fundamental *cause*.

In the next chapter, we will look at the Five Laws of Lean Design that you must leverage to solve your *Ility and Ing Equation*.

Lean Design Solution Tool

Tool Name: "As Is" *Ility* Checklist

Purpose:	Preliminary assessment of how your existing design is performing on the *Eight Primary Customer Ility Values*. Use as a checklist for making sure you clearly understand the "now" condition of your product before you begin to change it.
Steps:	1. Each stakeholder gives his perception of how well the current product is delivering value on all eight *Strategic Ilities*.

2. Stakeholders are encouraged to express their views as seen from their product domain — Design, Supply, Manufacturing or Customer Use.

3. Team leader collates responses and distributes summary to entire team

4. These opinions are used to begin discussion on where the new seat line should be improved.

Example: The example below is a passenger seat for use in a long distance, high speed passenger train. Current seat name is "Express." New seat will be introduced as the "Super Express."

Strategic Ility Values	Good	Needs Improvement
Performability	Seat exceeds all government safety requirements.	Seat recline failure a major customer complaint
Affordability	First class seat very cost competitive. Profit level excellent.	Budget seat cost 15 percent higher than competitor. Marginal profit on seat sale, profit made on service parts.
Featureability	Wide range of seats offered but very poor modularity and platform design	Optional features difficult to offer without redesign of product
Deliverability	Delivery good however customers demanding more JIT service	Some delays due to complexity of parts and quality of suppliers
Usability	Easy to service when an experienced maintenance person is on hand	Arm rest interference. Customers want more stable seat back trays
Maintainability	Design is best in the industry but room for improvement. Customers trying to drive down serviceability cost.	Growing complaints on serviceability time required. Many adjustments required. Seat was not designed for modular serviceability
Durability	We are considered to be the best in industry	We are not currently using some of the super-rugged materials now on the market
Imageability	Brand name leader in the train industry	Styling seen as being "out of date"

Summary

- The *Universal Lean Design Equation,* or simply the *Ility and Ing Equation,* states that a lean product design is one that *Optimizes Strategic Ilities, Minimizes Evil Ings.*
- *Ilities* are product values or attributes. *Ings* are tasks or process steps required to design, supply, manufacture and use a product.

- There are *eight primary values* all customers seek from a product. Likewise there are eight primary benefits your company wants from manufacturing a product. The *Lean Design Solution* uses these to begin solving the *Lean Design Equation.*
- All products are the sum of their lifecycle processes. Lean design requires a process view of a product design.
- The worst kind of factory cost is "hidden" from a design team's view. This is "indirect cost," "overhead," and "burden."
- The greatest opportunity for cost reduction is in your customer's domain. The *Lean Design Solution* helps you attack all types of cost, both visible and hidden.
- The *Lean Design Solution* is a Six Sigma quality tool.

Chapter 2

The Five Laws of Lean Design

In the last chapter, I described the *Universal Lean Design Equation* and why it is important for your lean product success.

In this chapter, I will begin to share with you the "how to" of solving that equation.

Five factors must be at work for your team to develop a successful lean design. These factors are as links in a chain.

All need to be strong. Ignoring just one of the five can be disastrous.

I call these the *Five Laws of Lean Design.* They are the most direct route to product value and simplicity.

> True innovation always arrives on the wings of simplicity.

These *Five Laws* give you the "true north" of what lean product design is all about. They also guide you the "how to" of making lean design really work for you.

Law of Strategic Value

Guides you in delivering the most important *Ility values* to all stakeholders along your product's entire lifecycle chain

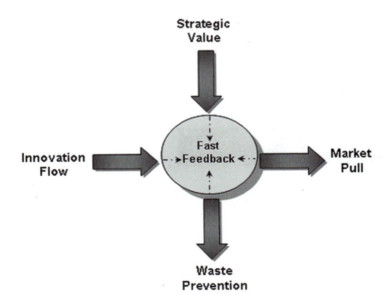

Law of Waste Prevention

Helps you prevent wasteful *Evil Ings* in every domain of your product's life *"from lust to dust."*

Law of Marketplace Pull

Shows you how to anticipate the three major forces of change that you must know in order to have the right products ready at the right time.

Law of Innovation Flow

Guides you in creating a stream of new ideas for delighting customers and differentiating your product.

Law of Fast Feedback

Shows you how to get the fast, meaningful feedback you need to make intelligent design decisions.

The *Five Laws of Lean Design* are easy to understand, easy to apply and easy to remember. But most important, they are the secret to great products.

First Law of Lean Design - *Law of Strategic Value*

This *First Law* governs the *Optimize Strategic Ilities* side of the *Lean Design Equation.*

The *Strategic Ilities* are the primary values your customer seeks in the product you are designing.

All customers seek *Eight Primary Values* from all products. If they are denied any of these, you are at risk of losing them as a customer

Your first challenge is to learn the specifics of what the customer needs from each of these *Primary Values.* They are your tickets to success.

Each of the eight are at too high a level to provide the detail your team needs to design your product.

> Your greatest enemy for tomorrow's success is sometimes today's success.

Their value lies in giving your team a gateway into the customer's mind.

Caution your design team against basing their overall design strategy simply on "requirements." They must go to the higher level of values before duck diving into specific requirements.

Values come first. Requirements come second.

Ility Owners as Team Members

Lean design requires that the "owners" of these *Ility* values be actively involved in creating the product design concept. Their needs must be part of the total design equation right from the start.

All four product lifecycle domains (design, supply, manufacture and customer) must be actively involved in order to understand the total challenge.

Product design is far more than identifying and integrating a product's technical requirements.

It's seeking, defining, solving, and integrating a product's total *business requirements throughout the value chain.*

Case in Point: Toyota takes special care to be open to new ideas from everywhere, both inside and outside their organization. The design process is seen not as the province of experts but a playing field for everyone.

They do this by seamlessly integrating knowledge beginning at the very start of their product development process.

Your company may not be able to directly mimic what Toyota does with its culture steeped in collaboration and deep technical experience. However, it is possible to use the techniques you learn here to attain the same results.

Good design always begins with problem seeking, not problem solving. Here are the questions that must be answered to assure you completely understand what a customer is seeking in each of these *Eight Primary Values*:

Questions You Must Ask

Primary Value	Customer Questions
Performability	What performance values are most important to the customer? How are these defined and measured?
Affordability	How does the customer define cost? How does the customer define value? What must we do to optimize cost without sacrificing what the customer considers to be value?
Featureability	Are there any product features, beyond basic values and requirements, which the customer may need but is not getting? Can we deliver features to differentiate us from the competition?
Deliverability	How does the customer define deliverability? How must we structure the product's architecture to make sure we meet the tempo of our customers demands?
Usability	How can we design the customer/product interface to minimize product learning and integration time?
Maintainability	How can we "chunk" our product to simplify serviceability or reduce the cost of "wear" components?

| Durability | How can we design our product so that it is impervious to the maximum level of human and environmental abuse? |
| Imageability | How can we create a deep sense of customer pride in owning and using our product? |

These questions are the *starting point* in building a value strategy customized to suit your product challenge. Each primary value must be fine-tuned to the point where it then meets your customer's specific needs.

You do not have to be best in all product value categories in order to defeat your competition. But you must be best in the *combination of those most important to your customer.*

The Primary Values Your Company Seeks

The *Law of Strategic Value* states that *your company* also seeks benefits from a product. This is in order to grow as well as pay shareholders a fair return.

Very importantly, how well your design teams respond to your company's primary values will determine the resources and support your management will give to your project.

One of your first tasks as a Lean Design Champion is to help your team completely understand this fact. Many good product design efforts have been abandoned because a design team ignored this part of the *Lean Design Equation.*

Your design team must be prepared to answer your management's questions about how your new design will benefit the company.

These are what I call management's "*Show Us*" questions.

Company Values Sought	Management's "Show Us" Questions
Profitability	Show us how your design will meet our profit goals. For example, how you are using techniques such as using existing parts and processes and low cost supply chain solutions to meet profit goals?

Investability | Show us how your product will be within our investment guidelines. How are you minimizing need for new investment by using such techniques as outsourcing?

Riskability | Show us how you are reducing risk by using proven design solutions and not introducing immature technologies. What is your process for risk analysis?

Produceability | Show us how you are involving manufacturing and suppliers "up front" to avoid production problems later. How are you minimizing new tooling and capital equipment?

Marketability | Show us the role marketing is playing on your design team. How will your new design will take advantage of existing sales channels or the cost of creating new ones?

Growability | Show us your design strategy for aligning your new product with our growth portfolio. What level of sales do you anticipate from this new product line?

Leverageability | Show us how you are designing your product to gain entry to new markets with high growth potential. How will the new product differentiate us from our competitors? Respectability Show how your product design will enhance our company's brand image and reputation for quality. Will it add luster and expand brand recognition?

Lean Design a Trade-Off between Values

Every product design requires trade-offs between these *Eight Primary Customer Values.*

Likewise, you must make constant trade-offs between *Customer Values* and *Company Values,* the ones your management seeks from your design effort.

In my early days in applying the *Lean Design Equation,* I used the words *"Maximize Strategic Ilities."*

But I was soon corrected. No design has ever been able to *maximize* all of these values, even when they are narrowed to a manageable set of six to eight *Ilities*.

What you can do is deliver the *optimum* set of values for your product opportunity. Optimum means the best solution possible. It does not mean 100 percent performance on each value.

These *Primary Values* give you a way to develop your *Lean Product Strategy*.

A product strategy is your high level, end-to-end approach for delivering value and reducing waste.

It's not a list of "requirements" or a timetable of events.

Developing such a strategy is your most important step. It captures the values your product will deliver to both your customers and company.

Strategic values set the direction your team will take in creating your product.

While your design drives 70 to 80 percent of all downstream product success, your *strategic thinking* will drive 80 to 90 percent of your team's ability to deliver that design.

The overwhelming majority of all new products fail due to a flawed product strategy.

Worst Product Development Waste is Failed Products

Over 60 percent of all new product development efforts are terminated before they ever reach the marketplace. Of the 40 percent that do make it out of the starting gate, less than half of these fail to become profitable or are removed from the market.

That means that *less than 20 percent* of new product design efforts really succeed.

Or in other words, 80 percent of all product development turns out to be waste.

This is *muda* on a grand scale!

And this math does not even begin to account for the waste of lost marketplace opportunity.

Missing an opportunity to grow and prosper is the greatest loss of all.

Yet I see design team after design team rushing to meet "requirements" without giving thought to developing an overall product value strategy. I have learned that these teams would have developed such a strategy if they had a process for doing so and if management required it to be done.

The *Lean Design Solution* was developed to give a design team what it needs to create an effective value strategy.

What is a Lean Design Strategy?

A *Lean Design Strategy* focuses your team on the six to eight essential values your product must deliver to be a success, both for your customer and your company.

In reality, your product design will have to deliver far more than these "strategic" six to eight values. However, these are the ones that are the most important for success.

Example: Affordability may be a key attribute your product must have.

However, *deliverability* may be just as important because if you cannot get it to market fast enough you will never be able to give your customer the low cost he needs.

No two product development efforts will have the same value strategy. If they do, then you most certainly know one of them is wrong.

This is because the forces of the marketplace are in a state of constant change. Marketplace conditions are always in flux. They are never exactly the same again.

Your strategy must be in tune with these forces of change and respond to them.

I will explain the *Three Forces of Change* when I cover the *Law of Marketplace Pull* later in this chapter.

Most important: Never use a tool that focuses on one *Ility* alone.

A good example is the use of Design for Manufacture and Assembly (DFMA) as the keystone methodology for your lean design effort.

As I recounted in the Introduction, you may end up optimizing the value on your factory floor, but sub-optimizing value your customer needs.

In short, you may be reducing factory *muda* but creating massive customer *super muda*.

Super Muda at Work

Consider a personal experience I had at one of my *Lean Design Solution* workshops.

During the morning break, an irate team member came up to me with a complaint. *"Did you,"* she asked impatiently,*" work with the Ariel (a fictitious automotive model) design team on that car's instrument panel?"*

I thought for a moment but then quickly answered, *"No...I worked on door panels and other interior components but never the instrument panel."*

"That's good," she replied. *"Because this morning I took my Ariel in for its usual service. As the service manager was going down my list, he came across my note to fix my instrument panel light."*

"He said, *'Miss, are you sure you want that light replaced?'* I replied, *'Of course! It can't be more than a few dollars.'*

"'No, Miss, fixing that light will cost you 250 bucks. You see, we have to remove the entire panel to replace it.'

"Those Ariel engineers may have designed that instrument panel for manufacturability but they sure didn't design it for serviceability!"

Moral of the story: Make sure you are working on all the right *Ilities* right from the start!

Coach yourself and your lean team members to think in a *holistic way.*

This means seeing the big picture, not just a part of it.

Six Rules for Building Your *Ility* Strategy

Here are six important ways to build your *Ility* strategy.

1. Start with the *Eight Primary Customer Values*. Begin at the beginning. Make sure everyone understands the concept of a "value strategy." Start with the *Eight Primary Customer Values* and then focus, define and calibrate them to the customers you are targeting.

2. Check your *Customer Value Strategy* against the benefits your company needs. Will you be able to deliver values to your company, given what the customer wants as value?

3. Get the input of all stakeholders. Invite all stakeholders to be part of the customer value definition process. If a stakeholder is not part of the customer value solution, he may become part of the delivery problem later.

4. Focus on the important or strategic few differentiators. Limit your strategic customer *Ilities* to no more than six to eight. That's about all a team can focus on at one time. Seek values that will differentiate you from your competition. However, don't disregard the other values you have to deliver.

5. Make sure everyone has the same definition. Use *Ility* words that lend themselves to unique definitions. This avoids confusion later.

Example: Microsoft uses the word "Lego-ability" to define the technology upgrade approach they want in all their products.

6. Remember that customer values never stop changing. Continually go back to your strategic values to make sure they are still valid. And remember that no two products will ever have the same value goals. Don't just recycle some other team's value strategy.

In Chapter Five, "Product Team Design Kaizan," I will take you through a process to accomplish all six of the above techniques.

Examples of Top *Ility* Thinkers

You don't have to look far to find examples of great *Ility* thinking.

Most agree today that lean value thinking did not originate with Toyota. And neither did lean manufacturing.

Lean manufacturing was flourishing in American companies while Toyota was still trying to figure out how to use it to build cars.

What the MIT book *The Machine That Changed the World* revealed was simply that Toyota was applying lean manufacturing *ahead of the auto industry.*

While America was not applying lean manufacturing to cars, it was using lean thinking in the "*manufacture*" and delivery of food.

The best example is Ray Kroc and his McDonald's empire. Kroc didn't use lean manufacturing words such as "takt time" or "customer pull" or "continuous flow" or "just in time."

But he clearly understood these concepts and used them to make himself a billionaire.

There are three lessons in the story I am about to share with you.

The first lesson shows the value of *looking outside your industry* for new ideas. Nothing much is new in the world today.

New ideas are simply unique combinations of old ideas.

The second lesson is the *power of story telling*. We humans learn best from stories.

The simpler the story, the easier it is to understand. As a Lean design champion use analogies everyone can understand, even though they may not directly be in your industry.

The third lesson is how Ray Kroc intuitively harnessed the *power of Ility thinking*.

Ray Kroc: Master *Ility* Thinker

When Kroc bought out the McDonald brothers' hamburger chain, he immediately added an ingredient to his menu that immediately differentiated him from his competitors.

Kroc began his empire in the period when wives were going to work full time. Time was limited. People wanted fast, dependable service.

He solved the first part of the lean design equation, *Optimize Strategic Ilities*, by adding the "ingredient" of speed, or *deliverability*.

Kroc is considered the "father of fast food."

What follows is an imaginary version of Ray Kroc's *Ility* strategy:

The Eight Primary Customer Values	Imaginary Version of Early McDonald's Strategy
Performability	Concentrate on consistency. Customers are highly mobile today and want the assurance that the product will be the same no matter at what store they may buy it.
Affordability	Be the leader in low priced food with an emphasis on "value." Use the word "value" to communicate that the product is not just about price.
Featureability	Offer various "side menu" items but don't drift too far from the core competency of delivering food fast with a limited menu.

Deliverability	Define deliverability by the number of seconds the customer has to wait for his food. Move from the metric of minutes to seconds.
Usability	Eliminate the need for any eating utensils. Enable the customer to add his own mustard, ketchup, etc. Make all packaging completely disposable
Maintainability	Design all stores to be the same. Drive toward perfection in ease of maintenance, food delivery and storage. Set rigorous "throw out" times for food. Durability Design all stores to have "robust" equipment built to McDonald's standards. Fool-proof all equipment. Never bring in new equipment without rigorous "off-line" testing
Imageability	Relentlessly promote the McDonald's "double arches" brand. Show "growability" by publicizing the number of hamburgers sold on every store's front sign.

At the same time, Kroc went to work on the second part of the equation, *Minimize Evil Ings.*

Kroc intuitively knew about the *Seven Gremlins of Waste.*

He applied the Second Law of Lean Design, *Law of Waste Prevention.*

This is the subject of our next section.

The Good Value Ility Brothers at Work

Lean Design Solution Tool

Tool Name: *Ility Checklist*

Purpose: Use the *Eight Primary Customer Ility Values* as a checklist for making sure you clearly understand customer needs.

Steps: 1. Each stakeholder gives his perception of how the customer defines each Strategic Value.
2. These are expressed as *Sub-Ilities* in perceived order of importance. List no more than eight *Sub-Ilities*.
3. Team leader collates responses and distributes summary to entire team
4. These definitions are used to begin agreeing on the most important values which must be met.

The example used below is for a passenger seat in a long distance, high speed passenger train.

Strategic Ility Values	Sub-Ility #1	Sub-Ility #2	Sub-Ility #3
Performability			
Affordability			
Featureability			
Deliverability			
Usability			
Maintainability	**Accessibility.** *Can reach any component for service within 60 seconds*	**Cleanability.** *Cleaning time 50 percent less than existing seat*	**Adjustability.** *No adjustments required during maintenance*
Durability			
Imageability			

Section Summary

- Balance the *Eight Primary Customer Values* against your company's *Eight Primary Product Benefits* to find the right combination of *Ilities*.
- Search for values in all four domains of a product's lifecycle: Design, Supply, Manufacture and Customer Use.
- Get the input of all stakeholders. If they are not part of the *Ility* strategy process they may become part of the implementation problem later.

- Seek *Ilities* that differentiate you from your competition.
- Limit your value equation to no more than six to eight *Ilities*. That's the maximum a product team can focus on at one time.
- Always revalidate your *Ility* strategy. Rapid marketplace changes could obsolete it at any time.

Second Law of Lean Design - *Law of Waste Prevention*

The *Law of Waste Prevention* states that every product design carries within it the *potential for creating waste from "lust to dust."*

There are *seven types* of design solutions that set in motion *most product waste.*

This waste appears throughout your product's lifecycle. The roots of waste begin to appear first in the design domain, then the supply domain, followed by the manufacture domain and finally, the most important domain, your customer domain.

> Men occasionally stumble over the truth, but most pick themselves up and hurry off as if nothing happened.
> — Winston Churchill

The *Law of Waste Prevention* addresses the second half of the *Lean Design Equation: Minimize Evil Ings.*

Your lean team's task is to minimize the use of these seven types of *Evil Ing* design solutions.

Lean manufacturing initiatives aim at *waste reduction.* However, the best solution is always *waste prevention.*

Knowing how to apply the *Law of Waste Prevention* will enable you to avoid design decisions that can create cost and quality problems later.

Why Improvement Efforts Start in the Manufacturing Domain

Quality initiatives and tools such as Six Sigma, statistical process control and lean manufacturing all started on factory floor.

Eventually, however, these initiatives inevitably shifted upstream to the product design stage.

Why do most product improvement initiatives always start on the factory floor?

The reason is that you can "count" product factory costs. Manufacturing processes are "real." You can see them, smell them and even hear them.

The arrival of lean manufacturing is bringing huge reductions in direct factory costs.

This time, however, the targets are the "hidden" factory costs. These are processes such as inventorying, storing, moving, checking and hundreds of others.

Value Stream Mapping (*VSM*) enables lean manufacturing teams to make waste visible.

VSM gives us a way to identify, map and eliminate waste, leaving only what is of value.

The tools and tactics of lean manufacturing have gone far in driving down the 50 to 80 percent of factory cost called "overhead." This kind of fire-fighting is paying off in highly visible and, most times, measurable results.

Inventory areas suddenly become smaller, available factory floor space grows, quality flaws are discovered quicker so re-work areas begin to shrink.

But eventually the low-hanging fruit is all picked.

It is at this point that companies remember that design is the primary driver of factory floor waste.

Their attention then turns to the design stage as they seek help in continuing their journey toward even leaner products.

Fire Prevention Much Tougher Than Fire Fighting

We are re-learning the lesson that factory floor cost and quality is the *effect phase* of bad design.

Design is the *causal phase*.

Fire-fighting factory floor waste is highly visual and can result in very quick wins.

Putting out fires always seems to get the spotlight.

But fire *prevention* is not a very heroic job. It's the sometimes dreary job of trying to stop problems before they have a chance to even start.

Carrying a child down the ladder from a burning building makes the headlines.

Inspecting buildings to make sure they meet safety codes doesn't even get a nod.

Why Waste Prevention Is So Tough

As you recall, *Ings* are all the processes and related tools, material and people that are required to deliver your product's values.

For example, in the *design domain*, these are all the actions required for *designing, prototyping, testing, qualifying,* and the many other tasks needed to develop a new design.

In the *manufacturing domain*, these *Ings* appear as *stamping, machining, grinding, assembling,* and hundreds more. These are the *Visible Ings* that accountants call "direct costs."

Direct costs are mainly the sum of your product's material and direct "touch" labor. These *Visible Ings* are well known by design teams.

Accountants provide design teams detailed cost information on these types of cost.

But today, *Visible Ings* are not the biggest cost problem.

They typically account for only 20 to 50 percent of all manufacturing product cost. This percentage continues to shrink every year.

Indirect corporate expenses, or "hidden costs," account for 30 to 75 percent of your total manufactured cost. These continue to grow every year.

I use the word "hidden cost" not because these don't end up on your company's balance sheet. I use it because these costs are *hidden from the view of your product design team.*

(I once had an irate accountant berate me for insinuating that his department was hiding expenses!)

Conventional Accounting of Little Help

Mass production accounting continues to fall behind as a way of revealing this kind of hidden cost in any meaningful manner.

Consider, for a moment, painting. Painting was traditionally considered a low cost process.

Ask an accountant what a refrigerator costs to paint and he will give you a dollar figure based on material and labor. This is usually a very small percentage of the total product cost.

But, what the accountant doesn't tell you are the specific hidden costs of painting. These are the hidden *Ings* of storing the paint safely. Then there is the prepping the painted surface.

And then there are the tasks of masking to avoid overspray, protecting both the environment and the people applying the paint, and packaging the painted surface so it won't be scratched.

On top of these *Ings*, there's retouching a damaged surface, removing the packaging and disposing of it, at the customer's site – just to name a few more.

The list goes on and on.

Painting is an *Evil Ing Gang* favorite. The Gremlins of *complexity, variability, sensitivity, dangerous* and *skill* are all hard at work.

Painting's hidden costs are many times the visible costs, and are the reason why it's on the "hit list" of many manufacturers.

The arrival of Activity Based Costing (ABC), with its unconventional technique of allocating total internal cost to individual product lines, has shed new light on real factory floor costs. But much of ABC cost information has been difficult to transfer to the early design stage.

ABC tells us a lot about specific product costs but very little about the specific *Ing* costs of those products. The information is still not in a format for helping product design teams assess complete costs.

> *Key Point: Lean Product Design gives us the chance to strike the Gremlins of Waste where they begin, before they even have a chance to do their damage.*

Indirect Costs Growing

Accountants define "indirect cost" as all dollars not directly linked to a product's physical "blue collar" labor or material content.

In this bucket go things like engineering tasks, supply chain management, factory floor supervision, inspection, plant facilities, materials management, information technology, sales and marketing and thousands more.

White-collar folks who do these jobs used to be at high risk as companies race to slash these costs either by "re-engineering," layoffs or outsourcing.

Now companies are getting smarter.

They are seeing the "driver" of many of these white-collar jobs as being product complexity, the number and types of processes required to design, manufacture, sell and support a product or service.

They are awakening to a simple fact: Just laying off white-collar employees does not eliminate the need to have these jobs done.

The downsizing binge of the past forced many of these "hidden cost" jobs to simply migrate to outside consultants or temporary employees. In fact, the consulting and temporary agency businesses have soared.

Smart companies are now trying a new approach. They are attacking the white collar cost problem at one of its major roots — product design.

Product development teams are now being challenged to design products that result in less white collar cost, not just blue collar cost.

Waste Prevention Skills Need Strengthening

However, there is a big stumbling block. Many product designers don't have a clue how to do this. Some have never been educated as to what these hidden costs are or what kind of design solutions create them.

Compounding the problem is the fact that even if a product team does make an attempt to reduce these costs, our mass production accounting methods cannot measure their success.

Traditional engineering teaches how to reduce "part" cost, the blue-collar element of the cost equation. Other than by simply reducing parts and hence reducing the costs of paperwork associated with that part, most product designers have little training in reducing a product's "hidden" cost.

So, like any problem left untended, white-collar product costs have skyrocketed.

In case any of this has the familiar ring of "attack problems at their root cause," it should. The "reduce hidden cost by design" movement is paralleling the great quality awakening of the past decade.

You can gain a competitive advantage by first identifying the "design drivers" of these costs in your company and then minimizing their impact "up front."

Customer *Ings* Greatest Opportunity

By far, however, the worst *Ings* a product design can create are those suffered by your customer. Like the hidden *Ings* on the factory floor, many times these are hidden from your product team's view.

Customer *Ings* include such things as *installing, learning, using, maintaining, servicing,* and *disposing.*

Your goal must be to simplify the product all along the lifecycle value chain.

As my wife says, a design is like a recipe. Some recipes are very complex. They have many different ingredients. They demand that you use many ingredients in a precise manner.

The number of different pots and pans for a complex recipe seems endless. And the time taken to prepare the product can be hours.

The result is sometimes just not worth the investment.

In the food industry, one of the biggest success stories today are frozen food entrees such as Lean Cuisine^{TM} and Smart Ones.^{TM} They minimize "hidden cost" while at the same time promising the values of nutrition and weight control.

The Seven Evil Gremlins of Waste Creation

As you recall from Chapter One, there are seven types of design solutions that set in motion most of a product's life cycle waste. These we call the *Seven Evil Ing Gremlins.*

The word "gremlins" comes from World War II when a constant stream of inexplicable "bugs" infested England's famous Spitfire fighter.

The Spitfire is perhaps one of the best known aircraft in the world. It is a flying legend.

The Spitfire's fame was born during the Battle of Britain. This was the attempt by Germany's Field Marshall Goering to gain mastery over British skies. Once gained, the Germans would launch their seaborne invasion.

The Spitfire was one of the keys to British success in that fateful summer of 1940. Germany failed and England was saved.

But pick up any history of World War II and you will read about how *gremlins* almost lost the battle for Britain. Disney even wrote a comic book about how this evil band almost brought down the Spitfire.

Only because of the hard, swift, behind the scenes work of English engineers were the *gremlins* eventually defeated.

Here is the real story.

The Spitfire was a single engine, low wing monoplane of monocoque and stressed metal wing construction. It was designed by the famous engineer, Reginald J. Mitchell of the Supermarine Aircraft Company.

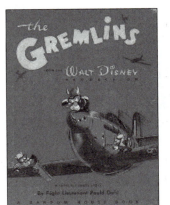

Its design was heavily influenced by Mitchell's earlier work on racing planes for international competition.

Though the Spitfire was a great success in terms of speed, it was not without its problems in *manufacturability, serviceability,* and *useability.*

This resulted in endless component failures that pilots chalked up to the *gremlins.*

Here is how the *gremlins* did their dirty work.

Complexity Gremlin

How it did its dirty work: Spitfire's complex, elliptical wing design required many different parts and processes. Each wing was almost hand crafted. There was a need for endless adjusting and hand fitting. Engineers worked hard to reduce this complexity and had developed simplified wing designs by the end of World War II.

Precision Gremlin

How it did its dirty work: The tolerances specified in the first design were at the limits of the factory's capability to deliver. Design for manufacture and assembly was initially not high on the design requirements. Deliverability was.

Variability Gremlin

How it did its dirty work: Each part was hand fitted to another. Assembly of the wings, as one designer put it, "was like a puzzle." This variability hampered fast repair in the field.

Sensitivity Gremlin

How it did its dirty work: Designed initially as a racer, the Spitfire had to be beefed up to take a beating in an air battle and still make it back to the base.

Immaturity Gremlin

How it did its dirty work: Virtually everything was new about the Spitfire, from its monocoque construction to its Rolls-Royce engines. Delivery of the first Spitfire was almost two years behind schedule.

Danger Gremlin

How it did its dirty work: Protection of the pilot was limited at first; however later models improved on this design flaw.

High Skill Gremlin

How it did its dirty work: The first Spitfires required high skill on the part of the pilot. However, later improvements made the plane a favorite among pilots, yet still a challenge for maintenance crews.

In the end the Supermarine engineers won their battle against the *Seven Gremlins of Waste*. The Spitfire went through hundreds of modifications during the war to defeat the *Seven Gremlins of Waste*.

The Spitfire ended up being the only airplane that had been in continuous production throughout the war — 20,351 had rolled off the assembly lines.

How Ray Kroc of McDonald's Minimized *Evil Ings*

In Chapter One, I described how Ray Kroc, founder of McDonald's, harnessed the power of strategic *Ility* thinking.

Ray Kroc was not only a great *Ility* thinker, he was also a master *Ing Buster*.

While I am sure Kroc never knew about the *Universal Lean Design Equation* or *the Seven Evil Ings of Waste*, he did have an uncanny instinct for eliminating complexity.

Here is an imaginary scorecard of how Kroc attacked the *Evil Ing Gremlins* in fulfilling the second half of his Lean Design Equation, *Minimize Evil Ings*.

How Ray Kroc and McDonald's Fought the Gremlins of Waste Creation

Complexity Gremlin

Strategy: Kroc relentlessly attacked complexity in any form. Original menus were very simple, thus minimizing customer selecting time, preparing time, and supplying time.

Precision Gremlin

Strategy: Machines, not humans, were given the job of delivering precision in the food value chain. McDonald's pioneered the use of automated systems to deliver the consistency for which they are famous.

Variability Gremlin

Strategy: A McDonald's hamburger in Boston tastes the same as one in Seattle. Kroc knew Americans were becoming highly mobile and wanted assurance that wherever they went to eat, the food would be the same. Kroc constantly worked on the McDonald's supply chain not only to deliver this consistency of quality but to drive down cost.

Sensitivity Gremlin

Strategy: Kroc knew he had to make food preparation, the customer interface, and his facilities "bullet proof" if he was to be successful in taking the McDonald's brand nation-wide. He constantly reiterated the McDonald's "design" to root out steps in that were sensitive to quality flaws.

Immaturity Gremlin

Strategy: While Ray Kroc was famous for experimenting to improve the McDonald's formula for success, this kind of tinkering was done off-line. Pilots were run to test new ideas and technologies. They were only brought on-line when fully proven.

Danger Gremlin

Strategy: Food consumption safety was, and continues to be, a primary McDonald's goal. Kroc knew that a bad experience in only one outlet could be heard across the United States. Rigorous standards were created to assure food consumption safety.

High Skill Gremlin

Strategy: Kroc knew that meeting the human labor challenge would be his toughest challenge, both in terms of cost and quality. His formula for success was based on minimizing human skill. This expanded the labor pool he could draw upon and, at the same time, assured the consistent quality he was seeking.

The Eight Rules of *Ing*

Every Lean Design Champion and design team must concentrate on being *Ing Busters*. Here are the *Eight Rules of Ing*:

1. **Be a *process thinker*.** A product's quality, cycle time and life span cost is the sum of its *Ings*, not its assembled parts.

2. **Reduce parts when it makes sense.** "Parts" are nothing more than integrated *Ings*. They are "Th-Ings." Begin your lean design quest by eliminating "Things" when it makes sense. When you eliminate a "Thing" you achieve a "No-Thing."

3. **Get design teams to think deeper than just part count reduction.** Fewer "Things" may not result in a better design. But fewer life cycle *Ings* always will.

4. **Invite those who are closest to the *Evil Ings* to join your design effort early.** Your product design sets in motion all lifecycle *Ings*. Get all the stakeholders who will be affected by the new product on board early. Show them the *Seven Gremlins of Waste*. Ask them to give you examples from their experience. Then get ready to take notes quickly. You will be surprised what they tell you.

5. **Think lifecycle.** A product's "manufacture-*Ings*" are typically far less than its total life cycle *Ings*. Look for *Ing* reductions where they will give you a competitive advantage. Look well beyond your factory floor.

6. **Work on complexity reduction first, cost reduction later.** Don't focus on reducing cost at your early design stage. Focus on reducing your design domain *Ings*. They are the root cause of all life cycle quality time and cost.

7. **Work on reducing the worst *Ings* first.** All *Ings* do not create equal pain. Some *Ings* create far more quality, time and cost problems than others. Create an *Evil Ing* score card to track your results.

8. **Relentlessly attack "hidden cost."** We have done a good job in driving down the "visible cost" of direct labor and material. Where we fail is in understanding and preventing the "hidden costs" along the product value creation chain. Begin this assault by looking in your *customer's domain* for opportunities.

Here is an *Evil Ing Thinking* conversion chart:

From...	...To
Complex	Simple
Precise	Adaptable
Variable	Consistent

Sensitive   Robust
Immature   Proven
Dangerous   Safe
High Skill   No Brainer

Lean Design Solution Tool

Tool Name: *Evil Ing Buster*

Purpose: Go problem finding before problem solving. Identify worst examples of *Evil Ings* in the "as is" design.

Steps: 1. Each stakeholder gives worst examples of how the "as is" design is creating *Evil Ings* in his domain.

2. Note: One example may be due to more than one *Evil Ing Gremlin.*

3. Team leader collates responses and distributes summary to entire team

4. These worst examples of waste are used to begin to focus the design effort.

Example: "As Is" *Express* passenger train seat

Evil Ing Gremlin	Design Domain	Supply Domain	Manufacturing Domain	Customer Domain
Complexity (Example)	Lack of product line standards. Constant new designing tasks required	Many different parts and processes. Too much sourcing required	Poor part commonality. Excessive stocking cost and handling time	Wear parts difficult to access. Servicing takes much skill and time
Precision				
Variable				
Sensitive				
Immature				
Dangerous				
Skill Intensive				

Section Summary

- Waste reduction and quality improvement initiatives typically start on the factory floor because the product takes physical shape there.

- However, most cost and quality problems originate from using one or more of the *Evil Ing* design solutions.
- Customer *Ings* such as installing, learning, using, and maintaining (among others) offer the greatest opportunity for capturing customer loyalty.
- Being an effective *Ing Buster* requires the ability to be a process thinker, one who can see well beyond a product's physical parts and imagine the hidden processes that product requires.
- Go to work on complexity reduction first and cost reduction later. A design team gets very little data on the worst kind of cost — "hidden" indirect expense.

Third Law of Lean Design - *The Law of Marketplace Pull*

The *Law of Marketplace Pull* guides you in predicting what *values* customers truly *need*, not only in the present time but in the future as well.

This *Third Law of Lean Design* says we must go well beyond the "voice of the customer" to find the customer's unspoken needs.

It says we must also listen closely to the voice of the non-customer.

But even more importantly, we must be reaching into the future to anticipate changing marketplace conditions that will create threats as well as opportunities for our product lines.

The *Law of Strategic Value* and the *Law of Waste Prevention*, explained previously, help us with this task. These two laws can be used as an organizing technique, or a checklist, for predicting future marketplace changes.

> There is nothing permanent except change.

While the specific *Sub-Ility* values customers seek will change over time, the strategic *Eight Primary Customer Values* do not.

The same is true for the *Seven Evil Ings* that create most product waste.

When you apply the full horsepower of the *Law of Marketplace Pull*, you will be able to:

- See emerging trends earlier than your competitors
- Fend off "disruptive" attacks by competitors more successfully

- Deliver customers product values when they want them and how they want them.
- Grow rapidly by discovering market niches and unmet needs to create your own disruptive strategy

Not knowing or applying the *Law of Marketplace Pull* can lead to completely missed opportunities and hasty attempts to "catch up," both of which can be disastrous.

Synchronizing Value Delivery with Value Demand

The term "marketplace pull" comes from the lean manufacturing practice of synchronizing production with customer demand. The customer "pulls" product forward. The goal of a lean manufacturer is to build products at that rate, not any faster, not any slower.

The opposite of this is the mass production idea of "product push" where products are built in large, supposedly economical, batches to await customer demand.

The *Law of Marketplace Pull* says the ideal product development pace is one that is synchronized with marketplace need. It should not be one that "pushes" products too early or too late or, worse yet, to a non-existent market.

Toyota calls this *"takt* time." The word *takt* comes from German and means "meter," as in musical meter.

Takt is the drumbeat of consumption by customers.

Likewise, the goal of lean product design is to have new customer products ready when the customer needs them, no earlier or no later.

> Nearly 50 percent of U.S. economic growth at the end of the 1990s came from lines of business that didn't exist a decade before.
> — *The Economist*

Is Product Development "Takt Time" Possible?

There are some who will tell you that such synchronization is impossible. Many believe there is no discernable rhythmic drumbeat to be heard.

They say the forces of "new product pull" are most times disconnected and chaotic, like an orchestra out of tune.

Examples given are competitors who suddenly introduce a new product. Or government regulations that suddenly change.

Or a new technology that suddenly emerges.

Hence some folks will tell you the lean concepts of *takt time* and *product pull* just don't fit the product development process.

Don't believe them.

Both concepts can be applied to product design. Toyota is superb at doing just that.

All of the above "sudden happening" events can be anticipated. They are predictable.

Three Sharks of Constant Change

To understand how to apply *takt time* or customer product pull, you must first be familiar with the *Three Sharks of Constant Change* and how they work.

These "sharks" begin to attack the competitiveness of any new product the day it is introduced — sometimes even sooner.

They guarantee that all products will begin their slide into obsolescence from the day they are conceptualized. No product or company is immune from the attacks of these forces.

You must be alert to them and be continually updating your product lines to survive their attacks. These sharks are circling your products constantly, looking for a weak spot.

The *Three Sharks of Constant Change* are:

Institute for Lean Innovation

Bart Huthwaite, Founder

P.O. Box 1999
French Outpost
Mackinac Island, MI 49757

Office: 906.847.6094
Fax: 906.847.6047
Cell: 248.705.6950

email: huthwaite@aol.com

The Marketplace

Customers are fickle. They are always demanding something new, less costly or with more features. Customers never seem satisfied, even when you have "listened to their voice" and delivered what they said they wanted.

We are now even more cautious when we listen to the "voice of the customers" as they are apt to change their mind tomorrow. And we must also be listening to the voices of the non-customers, those folks who have yet to use our products.

New Technology

Entire companies have changed almost overnight due to new technologies. New materials, processes and systems are continually challenging the dominance of mainstay products.

The internet forced Microsoft to entirely revamp its product strategy. Microsoft saw the Internet coming but reacted at only the last minute.

Competitors

This is the most vicious of the three "Sharks of Change." They are forever attacking your products with lower prices, more features, and faster deliveries.

Smart companies are willing to "attack themselves" first with new ideas. If you don't constantly come up with innovative products, you can be sure your competitors will.

Gillette is classic for "attacking" its own product lines. Gillette owns over 60 percent of the shaving blade market.

As marketing guru Jack Trout points out:

Every two or three years Gillette replaces its existing blade with a new idea. We've had two-bladed razors (Atra). We've had shock absorbent razors (Sensor). And now we have three-bladed razors (Mach 3).

A rolling company gathers no competitors.

The most challenging kind of competitor is the one who gains entry to your market by going after the low end of your customer base. The competitor then steadily moves up the product line until he is ready to take over your profitable business.

U.S. automakers saw this happen when Japanese manufacturers entered North American markets with low cost cars.

They then steadily expanded their product upscale to more profitable products and greater market share.

While these three sharks of change may seem to act independently of one another, there is a certain rhythm to their actions in every industry.

A good part of this rhythm is created by the market's ability to integrate, or "digest," new technology.

For example, the power generation industry has a fixed base of equipment, skilled employees and industry standards. The power generation's cycle of major change can be from seven to nine years.

This is in contrast to the toy industry that is highly flexible. The toy's industry's *takt time* for new products is one year or less.

There is one certainly: the time spans between major innovation shifts are rapidly shrinking.

Here are some examples of industry new product change *takt times*:

Industry	New Innovation Rate
Toy Industry	12 months
Computers	6-12 months
Automobiles	18-36 months
Gas Turbine Power Plants	7-9 Years
Navy Ships	12-18 years

Once in a while a Great White Shark comes along. The tragedy of September 11, 2001 created a sudden upsurge in the demand for security solutions. This was quickly followed by rapid experimentation with new types of security solutions.

The position you don't want to be in is to miss one of these drumbeats of change and then try to catch up.

What's even worse is to try to "leap frog" your competitor. You may end up in the pond short of the next lily pad or perhaps even beyond it.

Playing "catch up" ball can be painful and very risky.

Seize Opportunities Created by the Three Sharks of Change

While these *Three Sharks of Change* are always nipping at your heels, they are also creating market openings for you.

Change brings opportunity.

One of the best places to start to hunt for new opportunities is where the *Eight Customer Primary Values* are not being met or are being met poorly.

> The difficulty lies not so much in developing new ideas as in escaping from the old ones.
> — John Maynard Keynes

A good is example is why I am writing this book.

My observation is that there are thousands of lean manufacturing facilitators, Black Belts, and lean design implementation teams who are being asked to champion the cause of lean product design.

Yet as of this writing I have not been able to find an integrated method, techniques and tools to help them meet this challenge.

Many books address how to improve an overall product development process. Some talk about design for manufacturability and other specific *Ilities*. And some show how to improve the actual design process.

However, I can find none that offer a step-by-step way of designing a lean product that simultaneously optimizes value and minimizes waste across the entire product lifecycle.

This book is intended to fill that need.

Why Listening to the Voice of the Customer Can be Dangerous

Listening to the voice of the customer is important for meeting short term needs. However, the customer's "voice" typically tells us little about future needs.

> An optimist sees an opportunity in every calamity. A pessimist sees a calamity in every opportunity.
> — Winston Churchill

Anticipating the voices of your customers — as well as your non-customers — is equally important. By doing this you will be able to see the emergence of *disruptive* product opportunities and challenges.

Disruptive products are those that give customers values (*Ilities*) and reduce waste (*Ings*) in a way different from conventional product delivery strategies.

A successful product development strategy is one that is in harmony with marketplace demand. The challenge is to create products that neither *overshoot* nor *undershoot* that demand.

In order to do this you must be able to *predict* marketplace demand and, indeed, even *stimulate* it.

Separating "Wants" From "Needs"

At the heart of every great product is an unfilled need. If you can come up with a solution that meets that need, you have a winner.

A "need" is something a customer will pay money for. A "want" is something a customer thinks would be nice but may not go out of his way to pay for.

Kevin O'Connor in his book *The Map of Innovation: Creating Something Out of Nothing,* points to four questions that quickly separate a "want" from a "need."

1. Will the idea make the consumer or business money?
2. Will it save them money?
3. Will it make them more efficient?
4. Will it make them more competitive?

If the answer is no to all of these, you probably have a want rather than a need.

The most powerful kinds of needs are those that have to do with a fear of loss.

The idea of potential loss plays a large role in human decision making.

In fact, people seem to be more motivated by the thought of losing something than by the thought of gaining something of equal value.

What the three sharks take away, they also give.

They give you avenues to serve your customers better. That is, if you can recognize these opening before your competitors do.

Overshooting the Three Sharks: The *Vasa*

One of the worst mistakes is to *overshoot* the marketplace. Overshooting is when you deliver more in a product than the marketplace requires.

Or your product overshoots what is needed to defeat your competitors. Or it stretches the limits of the new technology you are trying to apply.

A classic example of "overshooting" is the seventeenth century Scandinavian warship *Vasa*.

It is now on display in Stockholm, undergoing restoration after resting on the bottom of that city's harbor since 1628.

That was when the *Vasa*, the most powerful ship ever built until then, sailed on its maiden voyage majestically to war only to sink within two miles of its dock.

It wasn't enemy cannonballs that brought the massive vessel to rest on the bottom of the harbor in 1628. It was faulty design.

This story begins with King Gustavus Adolphus. The good king was in somewhat of a pickle. His kingdom's long seacoast exposed his country to foreign attack.

European nations were eyeing Scandinavia for its vast mineral wealth. King Gustavus was worried. Scandinavia lagged well behind the other great nations of the time, especially England.

King Gustavus had a lot of catching up to do.

The king commissioned a ship to be built that would be the biggest and most advanced of its time.

His master shipbuilder jumped to the task and began applying the first and last of the Eight Primary Customer Values, *performability* and *imageability,* to the extreme.

The king saw bigger size and heavier armament as being the right answer to the *Law of Marketplace Pull* and the competitive threat that loomed before him. The ship was also designed to project an image of great naval sea power.

King Gustavus pressed the known limits of shipbuilding technology.

The *Vasa* was designed to be more than 220 feet long with masts 170 feet high. The ship's rudder stands over 30 feet tall.

This was much bigger and heavier than the ships England was building at the time.

Its triple laminated oak hull was built 18 inches thick.

The *Vasa* was definitely not environmentally friendly. Some of 40 acres of timber was used to build it.

The ship carried 64 cannons on two deck levels. The use of a second, lower gun deck and so many cannon was considered a technological feat for its time.

The experience required to build a ship of such heavy ship armament was completely unknown at the time.

As King Gustavus himself dictated the *Vasa's* requirements, no one dared challenge him about the feasibility of such a design.

The 64 cannons were heavily reinforced at the breech and weighed over 100 tons. *Vasa's* ballast equaled 120 tons of stone.

She carried additional weight of cannon balls, gunpowder, ancillary firearms, food in casks, officers and a crew of 133 sailors.

The design equation was definitely out of balance right from the start.

The first gun deck was almost at the waterline, exposing the ship to flooding. However, the shipbuilder had designed quick closing gun ports to prevent water from gushing in when the boat heeled to the wind.

Imageability was high on the value list. The ship was also designed as an artistic masterpiece. Its hull was adorned with carvings.

These were attached on the bow and round the high stern castle. Stern ornaments (painted red, gold, and blue) were carved gods, demons, kings, knights, warriors, cherubs, mermaids, weird animal shapes — all meant to scare the enemies and also symbolize power, courage and cruelty.

Forgotten in the ship's value equation were such attributes as *affordability*, *deliverability*, and, as was discovered early in its first voyage, *durablity*.

It took three intense years to build *Vasa*.

When complete she was a floating work of art and a powerful weapon of naval warfare. She was also riddled with *Evil Ings*.

It was if *Vasa* intentionally violated the *Optimize Strategic Ilities, Minimize Evil Ings* equation.

The ship designer's inclination to drive out the *Evil Ings* in order to improve quality was especially poor. The *Seven Gremlins of Waste and Poor Quality* lurked everywhere in her hull.

Here is how the *Vasa's* imaginary *Evil Ing* scorecard would look:

How the Seven Gremlins Infested the *Vasa*

Complexity

Shipbuilder attempted to integrate many new innovations all at the same time, including multiple cannon decks, excessive size, and use of large crew.

Precision

Gunports were designed to be a precision fit to prevent leakage while the ship was heeled over and underway. However, gunports could not be closed once excessive heeling started.

Variability

Coordination of sailing crew, gun decks, and officers on such a large ship was extremely difficult. Communicating orders on such a long ship while underway was almost impossible.

Sensitivity

Ship was very "tender" due to the lack of ballast to counter the weight of the 64 cannon, cannon balls, large crew and all supplies.

Immaturity

Exceeded the known limits of shipbuilding of the time re: ballast, use of multi-deck cannon. Crew on maiden voyage not well trained, had zero experience.

Danger

Seaworthiness dependent on how quickly the 64 gun ports could be closed. Failure to close only one could lead to sinking of the ship.

High Skill

The *Vasa* exceeded the ability of the crew to respond fast enough to close the cannon ports. The construction exceeded the skill of the shipbuilder's understanding of ballast.

As the ship passed before the Royal Palace of Stockholm, it began firing off proud salvos from its 64 brand new cannons. Suddenly a sudden squall caused the ship to list.

The *Vasa's* gun ports were still open having just fired farewell, and when she listed heavily to port, the gun ports sank below water level and water immediately gushed in.

The crew had no experience in closing the gun ports in such an emergency. The ship overturned almost immediately.

The shipbuilders didn't know how to calculate stability. They typically copied the measurements of other ships.

But the *Vasa* was an experiment and there was no model to follow for its size and second deck of cannons.

Since the lower cannon deck had to be above water, they didn't load enough weight into the bottom of the ship as ballast to offset the top-heavy warship.

In the king's quest to "leap frog" his competition, he had sailed into unknown waters.

And what about England, the king's potential competitor?

The pride of England's fleet, the *Mary Rose*, had sunk many years before due to a similar catastrophe. While anchored in harbor, a storm came up and water gushed in through her open gun ports.

While King Gustavus was moving in the direction of bigger ships and more armament, England was moving in exactly the opposite direction.

England was downsizing to smaller, faster, and more maneuverable ships that could be built more quickly and economically.

Moral of the story: Make sure you clearly understand where the *Three Sharks of Change* are really going before you begin your design.

And don't try to load too much innovation on your new product. You may sink yourself in the process.

Predicting the Sharks of Change

Following is a lean design team tool you can use to begin to learn what you do know — or don't know — about the Three Sharks of Change.

This tool is not intended as a substitute for rigorous market or technological research. It will, however, encourage asking the right questions about the quality of that kind of effort.

And, very importantly, it will enable market researchers and technologist to directly participate in a product design effort.

The *Three Sharks Prediction* tool will also show management how well your team has considered product migration in your design strategy.

Applying the *Law of Marketplace Pull* helps us understand the shape of the future. However we must also be prepared to meet the future with innovative solutions.

That requires applying the *Law of Innovation Flow.* This is the subject of the section that follows.

Lean Design Solution Tool

Tool: *Three Sharks Prediction Tool*

Purpose: Help a lean product team design its product to be robust enough to meet future marketplace needs.

Participants: Entire product team as well as market research and technologists.

Process: Individuals first calibrate time spans between Step, Stretch and Leap. They then write their predictions from their functional (marketing, manufacturing, etc.) point of view. They then share their thoughts with the team. Open issues and conflicting opinions are recorded and assigned to individuals for follow-on work.

Three Sharks Prediction Tool Typical Questions

Marketplace

Step (First Generation): Does your design strategy address all the *Eight Primary Values?* Are you delivering too much? Too little?

Stretch (Second Generation): What are the top five to seven changes you anticipate in your customer's *Eight Primary Values?*

Leap (Third Generation): Are there any "disruptive" marketplace changes on the horizon?

Technology

Step (First Generation): Does your design take advantage of all existing technology? Are you *pushing* the technology too far?

Stretch (Second Generation): What new technologies do you anticipate emerging? Do you have the capability to develop these internally?

Leap (Third Generation): Are there any "disruptive" technologies emerging in the distant future that could obsolete your entire business?

Competition

Step (First Generation): How competitive are you today? What are your differentiators?

Stretch (Second Generation): Are there any new competitors who may try to enter your market space by offering a "simplified" solution compared to yours?

Leap (Third Generation): Would a merger of competitors endanger your market position? Are overseas producers a threat?

Section Summary

- The *Law of Marketplace Pull* helps you to *anticipate* what values your customers will seek in the future.
- The *Laws of Strategic Value* and *Waste Prevention* can be used as a framework for predicting those needs.
- Product development must be synchronized with marketplace need.
- *Undershooting* is not delivering the right value when needed. *Overshooting* is delivering too much. One can be just as bad as the other.
- There are three forces of change that begin to obsolete all products immediately. These *Three Sharks of Change* are customer needs, new technology and your competitors.
- The emergence of change is predictable. The *Three Sharks of Change* can be used as a framework to conceptualize both the pace and kind of change that will occur.

Fourth Law - *The Law of Innovation Flow*

Each year I speak on the subject of product innovation before thousands of people.

I encounter many who are convinced product design today is so complex that it is well beyond the capabilities of non-technical folks.

I've heard these "too complex" words many times from integrated product team members who are not engineers.

Nothing could be farther from the truth.

In reality, design is really a very simple process.

In fact, some of the *best* ideas come from people who have the *least* design experience. Great "out of the box" thinking can come from people who don't even know there is a box.

> Expect the unexpected or you won't find it.
> — Heraclitus, Greek philosopher

What is lacking is a *systematic way* for everyone to contribute innovative ideas.

This is where the *Law of Innovation Flow* comes into play.

The *Law of Innovation Flow* states that we must provide a way for all members of an integrated design team to participate in the innovation process.

Only by seeing the design challenge from many different perspectives will we ever be able to solve it.

The *Law of Innovation Flow* also states we must begin to develop products well ahead of when the marketplace will need them. Getting ready for the future has to start in the present.

Product values will inevitably decay. They will always require continuous improvement to remain competitive.

In this section you will learn how to *systematically* find new benefits in order to deliver a *continuous stream of value* to your customers.

It is the "seeking of perfection" that lean manufacturing champions are always espousing on the factory floor. The same holds true for the design phase.

No product design can ever perfect. All designs are compromises between functions, cost, time and endless other factors. So imperfection is a constant in all product designs.

When we apply the *Law of Innovation Flow*, we are able to:

1. Fully explore the *Five Improvement Targets* that every product offers
2. Apply the *Eight Lean Design Tactics* to improve those product targets

3. Systematically find new design solutions never uncovered before
4. Deliver the right product values to customers at the right time
5. Show why everyone is capable of being a lean product innovator

Use "Systematic Innovation"

Good lean design teams practice what I call *systematic innovation.* This is the willingness to turn over every rock of opportunity before giving up the quest for new ideas.

I find that product design teams who do poorly at innovation typically suffer from one of two maladies. The first, and the most common, is the compulsion to keep their search for new ideas to a minimum.

Such a team either sets the constraints, or boundaries, of their design playing field so tightly than not much in the way of new ideas emerges. Or they set very short time limits on their quest which has the same effect.

The second malady is the team "opens up the box" and goes on a wide ranging brainstorming journey into far fields that don't offer a ghost of a chance for success.

Setting your design space too broad is just as bad as having it be too narrow.

The Five Targets of Opportunity

The *Lean Design Solution* says that every product offers *five targets of innovation opportunity.*

- **Functions.** Purposes the product is designed to deliver across its total lifecycle.
- **Parts.** Subsystems, modules, components and tools needed to deliver the product's functions.
- **Processes.** Tasks required for delivering the product's functions or creating its parts across the product's entire lifecycle.
- **Materials.** Materials required for manufacturing the product's parts. These can also be the expendable materials needed to use the product, such as fuel.

- **People.** The number of humans and their expertise needed to design, manufacture, install, use, service and dispose of the product.

All five of these elements offer virtually endless opportunity for improvement.

Unfortunately, many product teams fail to fully explore all of these targets.

The typical brainstorming practice is to look first at changing *functions.* This is usually followed by an effort to reduce *parts* or simplify *material* specifications.

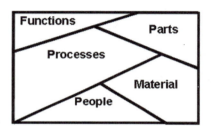

Five Targets of the Lean Product Puzzle

In reality, the last two elements, *processes* and *people,* may carry a far greater potential for innovative thinking than the first three. One of the reasons why they are not explored fully is that they are difficult for the design team to visualize.

An engineering drawing or sketch will clearly reveal functionality, material specifications and part geometries. Yet it will say little about the complexity of the processes required.

And it communicates very little about the human expertise required to manufacture and use the product. Unknown problems or those that are difficult to understand are seldom solved.

That is why looking at a product design through the lens of the *Seven Evil Ings* is such a powerful technique.

It reveals a design's potential for *process complexity.*

Three Levels of Opportunity

Creative ways to change these *Five Targets of Opportunity* can be explored on *three primary product levels.*

System. The product's highest level of integration. In the sketch below it is the complete automobile.

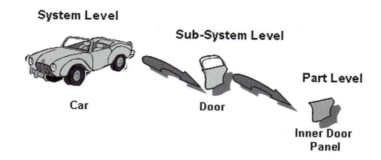

System Level

Sub-System Level

Part Level

Car

Door

Inner Door
Panel

Sub-Systems. Sub-assemblies that make up the total system. In this example the sub-system is the car door.

Parts. The individual components that make up sub-systems.

Think Backwards From the Future

Many years ago I started using a technique I now call *Backwards from the Future*. It has worked so well that it is now a major component of the *Lean Design Solution*.

Here is how it works. Your design team starts its innovation quest by imagining what shape the Five Targets might take many years in the future.

Seeing the *Five Targets* forward in time expands our creative thinking. It also prepares us for the future.

The continuous onslaught of the *Three Sharks of Change* — customer, technology and competitor —

> Methodical innovation is not an oxymoron.
> — Kevin O'Conner, author of *The Map of Innovation*

requires that we think about our product in not only the present tense but in the future tense as well.

Not thinking about how we will have to modify the product in the future can lead to a costly blind alley.

The *Lean Design Solution* uses three generations, *Step-Stretch-Leap*, as the framework for doing this. These are:

- **Step Generation.** This is the product design for the immediate future
- **Stretch Generation.** This is the design-after-next.
- **Leap Generation.** This the design of the distant future

This kind of *Step-Stretch-Leap* thinking prompts your design team to anticipate changes in the marketplace of the future. It brings the *Three Sharks of Change* directly into your lean design equation.

Thinking about future solutions helps us anticipate technology shifts, marketplace changes and, very importantly, your competitor's strategies.

This kind of *Backwards from the Future* thinking also surfaces problems early. It reveals resources that will be needed.

The best way to begin design thinking is with the *Leap* generation. Working backwards from an ideal future solution frees our minds from the constraints of the present.

Seeing the Future in the Present

Here is an imaginary look at how an automotive engineer might have used this kind of *Step-Stretch-Leap* thinking a decade ago.

Car Door	Step now	Stretch + 5 years	Leap + 10 years
Functions	Integrate automatic window lift into door	Integrate seat adjust, window lift, door lock functions into inner door panel	Integrate inner door panel with door structure, including all previous functions
Material	Wrap fiberboard inner door panel with vinyl	Mold inner door panel as one part using engineered plastic	Integrate inner door panel and outer shell by using composite material
Parts	Eliminate screws and washers securing inner door by using plastic push fits	Eliminate push fit fasteners by integrating snap fits into plastic inner panel	Eliminate all fasteners with totally integrated door and inner door
Processes	Reduce screw inserting and securing with plastic push fits	Eliminate assembly of push fits to inner door	No assembly processes required
People	Parts stocking, manual assembly reduced	Only one human assembly step required	Automatic assembly. No human labor required

Benefits of Step-Stretch-Leap Thinking

Step-Stretch-Leap thinking expands the playing field of your team's collective mind. When you visit the future in the present, the number of opportunities that begin to unfold will startle you.

Here are some benefits:

- **Open-Ended Thinking.** You liberate your thinking, and that of your team, from the constraints of today.
- **Gain an Advantage.** You can see targets of opportunity quicker than your competition.
- **Strategic Alignment.** You can develop an aligned portfolio strategy for your entire product line across multiple generations.
- **Avoid Re-Inventing the Wheel.** You can avoid "blind alleys" and having to "start from scratch."
- **Stronger Stakeholder Participation.** You can get active participation of marketing, R and D, and virtually all your company's stakeholders, as well as customers in this "seeing the future" approach.

Step-Stretch-Leap thinking does not require that you have all the answers. It does force you to ask all the right questions. This is the first and most important step in finding the right answers.

To learn more about this kind of future thinking, read the excellent book *The Minding Organization* by Moshe F. Rubinstein and Iris R. Firstenberg (John Wiley and Sons, New York, 1999).

Why Innovation Is "Everybody's Job"

Gaining strong stakeholder support begins with making all stakeholders "part of the solution" rather than "part of the problem."

Getting all stakeholders into the innovation game brings many different perspectives to the table.

Here are three reasons why innovation must be "everybody's job" on a lean product design team:

- **Strong Buy-In.** When a stakeholder is part of the innovation process, their level of "buy-in" and support is far stronger than if they were not part of the process. As the old saying goes, *"It is very difficult to call your own baby ugly."*

- **Systems View.** A total "systems view" is possible when you have all stakeholders playing a role. It is very difficult for marketing to understand engineering's issues and vice versa.
- **Creative Ideas.** Great ideas can sprout from anywhere. Many of the most astounding inventions originated in the minds of "non-inventors."

Innovation is a Game Everybody Can Play

In my library is a famous book by the English author James Burke. Burke gave the world the astounding book *Connections*. Made into a television series a number of years ago, Burke's book combines popular science with a little Sherlock Holmes detective work. His book retraces the steps that led to eight major inventions.

These eight inventions ushered in the technological age. They are the computer, the production line, telecommunications, the airplane, the atomic bomb, plastics, the guided rocket, and television.

Burke explains:

> *As each story unfolds it will become clear that history is not, as we are so often led to believe, a matter of great men and lonely geniuses pointing the way to the future from their ivory towers.*
>
> *At some point every member of society is involved in the process by which innovation and change comes about, and this book may help to show that given average intelligence and the information available to the innovators of the past, any reader could have matched their achievements.*

My experience mirrors Burke's observation. I have discovered that when given some basic principles, design tactics and common sense rules, *anyone* can be an innovator.

Your Inventive Role

Innovative design can be simply the application of common sense to an unseen problem.

Non-experts sometimes have the advantage of not being constrained by the accepted wisdom. Not knowing "that's just the way it is" or "that was tried once but failed" may help the non-expert find new ideas that the expert would not have discovered.

Read what Barry Nalebuff and Ian Aryes found in writing their innovative book *Why Not? How to Use Everyday Ingenuity to Solve Problems Big and Small.*

> *Innovations are not just top down, but bottom-up and sideways. It's easier to think outside the box when you don't know where or what the box is.*

Take for example the case of Bette Nesmith. She was the inventor of liquid paper.

Bette (mother of the Monkee's Mike Nesmith) was happily working as a secretary when she wondered why artists could paint over their mistakes, but typists could not.

Using her kitchen blender, Bette mixed up a batch of water-based paint to match the company stationery and poured it into an empty nail polish bottle. She then took it to work. Using the small brush, she could paint over and fix typos.

Some 28 years later, Gillette bought her company for $48 million.

Invention is human nature

I believe that most of we humans have an inherent desire to "invent." We are always conjuring up different ways to do things better. It is only with the advent of the corporate structure that "design" was turned over to a small band of technicians.

The emergence of the Integrated Product Development team with its multi-functional membership is helping us return to our design roots.

Even small ideas can have a big effect. "The Butterfly Effect" beautifully illustrates why you should always welcome all new ideas, no matter their immediate impact.

In 1963, meteorologist Edward Lorenz announced a stunning theory.

For decades, people had viewed the universe as a large machine in which causes matched effects. People presumed that big causes had big effects, and little causes produced little effects.

Lorenz doubted this.

The question posed to Lorenz sounded strange but simple: Could the flap of a butterfly's wings in Singapore start a wind in motion that became a hurricane by the time it reached North Carolina?

After considerable study, Lorenz answered yes.

Lorenz's theory of what is now called the Butterfly Effect was one of several findings in the last twenty years that reflect the unpredictability of everything: from weather to the outcome of product development programs, and the distant but often enormous effects of tiny causes.

Many people, however, were not surprised by Lorenz's discovery. These were those folks who had witnessed this kind of "small-effects-can-have-major consequences" phenomena first hand.

For example, everyone in the industrialized world today benefits from microwave cooking.

Very few know, however, that Percy LeBaron Spencer, a physicist at Raytheon, invented the microwave oven after accidentally melting a candy bar in his pocket with microwaves during one of his research projects.

This is a world where tiny changes can often produce enormous effects.

Innovation Requires Positive Mindset

Pessimists don't make great product designers. Positive thinkers do.

Here is a collection of my favorite quotations. You may want to use them when your design team gets stuck.

"A conclusion is a place where you get tired of thinking."
— Edward DeBono, innovation guru.

"The amount a person uses her imagination is inversely proportional to the amount of punishment she will receive for using it."
— Roger von Oech, creativity consultant

"Now is no time to think of what you do not have. Think of what you can do with what there is."
— Ernest Hemingway

"Your idea needs to be original only in its adaptation to the problem you are currently working on."
— Thomas Edison

"Who the hell wants to hear actors talk?"
— Harry M. Warner, Warner Bros., 1927

"Sensible and responsible women do not want to vote."
— Grover Cleveland, 1905

"Heavier than air flying machines are impossible."
— Lord Kelvin, President, Royal Society, 1895

"Everything that can be invented has been invented."
— Charles H. Duell, Director U.S. Patent Office, 1899

"There is no likelihood man can ever tap the power of the atom."
— Robert Millikan, Nobel Prize in physics, 1923

"Babe Ruth made a big mistake when he gave up pitching."
— Tris Speaker, baseball player, 1921

Urgency as the Mother of Invention

Want to know the secret to a successful invention? Don't look for "wants." Look for "needs."

Especially look for a urgent need that requires a quick solution. As I always remind design teams of the *Rule of the Itch*:

Find a customer itch and scratch it quickly. You will move to the head of the line for solving all other itches that arise.

Need combined with urgency is a powerful incentive for change. We are not highly motivated to change our ways when we don't perceive an immediate need for doing so.

Even when our logic tells us that we must change, we are typically slow to do so.

Take for example the case of Chrysler Corporation. Smaller than its American competitors, Ford and General Motors, Chrysler got into hot water a number of years ago when the automotive market was in a tailspin.

Chrysler was on the brink of bankruptcy. Ford and General Motors logically knew they had a need to downsize and change, however the urgency to do so was not as high as it was at the smaller Chrysler.

Shocked by its precarious predicament, Chrysler reacted rapidly and launched a series of changes that carried them through the crisis and enabled them to be stronger in the long run.

Complacency at Ford and Chrysler set in after the crisis passed.

A friend of mine and a senior Chrysler executive during the crisis explained Chrysler's response to an urgent need this way:

> *We were like the frog thrown into a boiling pot of water. A frog's reflexes are so fast that can leap out of that boiling water without even scalding his thin skin.*

> *However, take another frog and put him into a pot of luke-warm water and he will happily enjoy his swim. Then, ever so gradually, turn up the heat and the frog will allow himself to be cooked for a meal.*

> *We were like the first frog. We had an urgent need to change. General Motors and Ford were like the second frog. There was a need but no urgency.*

Seek Many Solutions

Someone once said, "There is nothing as dangerous as an idea when it is the only one you have." I urge design teams to use what I call the *Rule of Iteration*. It goes like this:

**Your first design is never the best,
the second and third only a step
in your journey to success.**

You will never get it right the first time at bat. Think in terms of many solutions, not just many ideas.

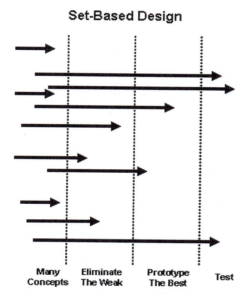

Set-Based Design

Many Concepts · Eliminate The Weak · Prototype The Best · Test

Toyota has one of the most successful product development organizations in the world. Academics and practitioners alike attribute much of their success to what is called *set based concurrent engineering.*

This is the practice of looking at many different kinds of design solutions, or "sets," before making a final choice. Many solutions sets are carried well into the prototype stage before this final selection is made.

The practice of set-based engineering begins by clearly mapping the solution space and broadly considering sets of possible solutions. These are gradually narrowed to converge on a final solution.

Casting a wide net from the start, and then gradually eliminating the weak or risky solutions, makes finding the best solution more likely.

"Keep your options open as long as possible" is the motto of this kind of design team.

While at first glance you may this means unnecessary expense, Toyota doesn't think so. The prototype designs that are not selected may be usable at a future date.

Or some of the knowledge gained from them can be very useful in terms of what *not* to do.

Knowledge has a high value at Toyota. The data gained from such advanced prototyping is carefully documented and made available to all engineers.

Point Based Design

In contrast, many American manufacturers pursue what is called *point based* product development. Point based design has a team looking at several different concepts.

But then the team is urged to quickly converge on one solution, a single point in the design space, and then modify that solution until it meets the design objectives.

Point-Based Design

There is little experimentation on the front end. The idea is to fix on one solution path as soon as possible.

This seems like a very cost-effective approach unless one finds they have picked the wrong starting point solution. Reworking a single design solution can be very time consuming and frustrating.

It can even lead, in many cases, to a sub-optimal design

The *Lean Design Solution* is a set-based design methodology. One of the most common complaints about looking at many different design solutions is that there is no accurate way or enough time to compare many designs at the early product development stage.

The *Lean Design Solution* solves this problem by giving you a way to compare many designs quickly. This technique is based on the *Law of Fast Feedback*.

This is the subject of the section that follows.

Lean Design Solution Tool

Tool: *Innovation Flow Tool*

Purpose: Help a lean product team design see how the five elements of all products might change in the future. This tool provides a framework for "thinking from the future to the present."

Participants: Entire product team as well as market research and technologists.

Process: Individuals first calibrate the *takt* time spans between Step, Stretch and Leap. They then write their predictions. They then share their thoughts with the team.

Car Door	Step Now	Stretch + 5 years?	Leap + 10 years?
Functions (example)	Integrate automatic window lift into door?	Integrate seat adjust, window lift, door lock functions into inner door panel?	Integrate inner door panel with door structure, including all previous functions?
Material			
Parts			
Processes			
People			

Section Summary

- The *Law of Innovation Flow* states that you must develop products in multiple generations in order to be prepared for the future.
- Every product offers *Five Targets of Innovation Opportunity.* These are: *functions, parts, materials, processes* and *people.*
- The *Five Targets* can be explored for creative solutions on three primary levels — *system, sub-systems* and *parts.*
- *Backwards from the Future* thinking is a Lean Design Solution for freeing up your design team's collective mind. It also surfaces problems early so that they can be solved in a timely manner.
- *Step-Stretch-Leap* design is a framework for thinking about products in a multi-generation mode.
- Innovation is everybody's job. You don't need to be an expert. When your entire team plays in the innovation game, you have many more new ideas and stronger buy-in.
- Innovation can simply be asking a question never asked before.

- Pessimists make poor inventors.
- Set-based design is looking at many different "sets" of design solutions at the same time as you move through your product development phase.

Fifth Law - *The Law of Fast Feedback*

The *Law of Fast Feedback* says you can only improve what you can measure.

Measurement helps you bring a strong sense of direction and clarity to your lean product design effort.

But be careful.

We will get what we measure. Measure the wrong things and chances are you will get the wrong results.

We should be measuring what matters most.

I find that most product design metrics don't really reflect the product game plan.

Measurement is one of the weakest areas in product development today.

"Real time" metrics help us most. They tell us how we are doing while we are still early enough in the design phase to take corrective action.

But ask a design team what real time metrics they are using and you probably will quickly get the answer:

"Schedule, budget and technical performance."

While these three are important, they are far from being enough.

We must measure how well we are solving the equation *Optimize Strategic Ilities, Minimize Evil Ings.*

Recall that *Strategic Ilities* are the key six to eight customer values that must be the focus of your design effort.

Evil Ings are the seven types of design solutions that create havoc with cost and quality.

Measuring your product's *Ilities* and *Ings* brings clarity to what matters most for your success.

The *Lean Design Solution's* measurement method you will learn in this book gives you a way to convert these *Ilities* to a set of measurable outcomes.

Most Common Failures

Measurement systems have one of the highest failure rates of all corporate initiatives.

Why do measurement systems fail so often?

In their classic study of measurement systems, *Measure Up! Yardsticks for Continuous Improvement,* Richard L. Lynch and Kelvin F. Cross boiled down complaints into a few common themes.

- **Out of Tune Metrics.** Measurement feedback is not specifically tuned to your product design game plan. The measurements may yield irrelevant or even misleading information. Worse yet, they may be provoking behavior that undermines the product goals.
- **System Sub-Optimization.** The use of a feedback system that tracks each dimension of product value separately, thus distorting how effectively the product as a whole will perform as a system
- **Internally Focused Metrics.** Metrics that are solely focused on internal performance (Design for Manufacture and Assembly) as opposed to also measuring the perspectives of the customer (Design for Maintainability, etc.)
- **Tardy Data.** Financial metrics that come too late for mid-course corrections and remedial actions.
- **Punishment Rather Than Learning.** The primary purpose of measurement is to get feedback. Some measurement systems, however, are used like a teacher's rule in the classroom. They are used for punishment rather than to promote learning.
- **Inflexibility.** Inflexible and rigid metrics. The best measurement systems are flexible. They are "more a tape measure than a rigid ruler."

One of the greatest causes of flawed designs is early *dollarization.* This is the notion that if a product benefit cannot be expressed in dollars, then it is not valid.

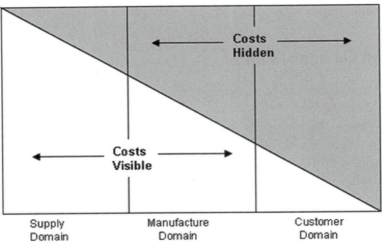

Product Cost Knowledge Wedge

For example, many design decisions are made solely on the basis of the visible direct cost. Indirect or "invisible costs" are not considered as they cannot be quantified in dollars.

The end result is that direct costs may be reduced but indirect costs increased.

In reality, knowledge about product costs *decreases* as it migrates through its lifecycle domains.

When components arrive from the *Supply Domain,* most costs are quite clear. They are shown on the supplier's invoice. Accounting systems shows this cost very accurately to the design team

When these components are integrated with additional components and work in the *Manufacturing Domain,* the total cost begins to get muddy. Overhead costs are typically applied across a broad range of product types. Only the direct costs can be known with any accuracy.

But the total cost picture becomes most unclear when the product enters the *Customer Domain.* Many design teams can have a very limited view at this point.

The *Lean Design Solution* gives you a way to overcome these problems. It helps you create a feedback system that delivers the right information to you at the right time about the *root cause drivers of cost.*

It is a method that is complete, yet flexible enough to be used with an endless range of products and services.

In this section I will focus on giving you a "thinking model" for harnessing the full horsepower of measurement in product improvement.

In Chapter Five, "Lean Design Scorecards," you will then learn the mechanics of using "spider charts" to create scorecards for making design decisions.

Predictive Feedback is Tough

As we look at ways to deliver the values our customers seek, we need a method to help us understand how well we are doing on each of the *Strategic Ilities*.

We need to know (1) where we are now, (2) where want to go, and (3) how well we are progressing in getting there.

All measurement systems require these three elements.

For example, you need to fly to Los Angeles and you are now in Boston. You might know the global positioning satellite (GPS) coordinates of Los Angeles down to one foot.

However, if you did not have the GPS coordinates of Boston, you may end up heading east instead of west.

The next thing we have is *feedback:* how well we are moving toward our goal.

Too often a design team maps a new product course but forgets to take along a compass to make sure they are on the right track. What they need is *performance feedback.*

Feedback is the mechanism we look to for taking corrective action. The *Law of Fast Feedback* says that you must have a system for knowing when you are on course and off course. It says that without feedback there can be no useful improvement.

The right kind of feedback will bring knowledge, understanding and direction. The wrong kind of feedback, or the absence of any feedback, can drive your lean design effort off course.

What makes product design measurement so tough, however, is that the time dimension between when we make our design decisions and the time when the result is actually known can be many months, years or even decades.

In order to fill the gap between this huge *cause and effect span* we must rely on *predictive feedback.*

Predictive feedback tells us the likelihood our decisions will have the desired results.

Three Benefits

A design team benefits from creating a predictive feedback system in four important ways:

Gets everybody is on the same page. Completing a journey is difficult if all the stakeholders have a different idea as to the destination. Measurement provides focus, direction and a common understanding of the product team's goals.

Helps you make more enlightened decisions. Predictive feedback gives you knowledge needed to make good decisions. The more you understand the cause and effect relationship between your design actions and the later results, the more effective those decisions will be.

Strengthens buy-in and implementation. Data driven, measurable design solutions generate better understanding and stronger support. Implementation becomes easier. Resistance becomes less.

Right Kind of Data Needed

Writing in their excellent book, *Measuring Organizational Improvement Impact,* Richard Y. Chang and Paul DeYoung find that the worst kind of measurement system is one that is a DRIP…"Data rich and information poor. "

Or in the words of Samuel Taylor Coleridge's famous line, *"Data, data, everywhere, and none to help you think. "*

Many product design feedback systems fail because they generate loads of measurement detail that is not *actionable* by the design team.

For example, the product team may get endless maintenance records from the field, yet no systematic "root cause" analysis of why failures are occurring.

Most failures, including costly maintenance, can be traced to one or more of the *Evil Ings* I discussed earlier.

Seven Rules for Effective Feedback

How effective are the metrics you currently use? Do they give you the feedback you need to deliver the right value at the minimum cost?

Here are seven rules for effective measurement and feedback. I gathered them from the experiences of hundreds of companies throughout the world:

Feedback Rule #1. Measure what is most important to your customer, not just what is easy to measure.

Remember that the three most common "in process" metrics used by a design team are (1) schedule, (2) technical performance and (3) cost or budget are essential. However they are only the beginning of a good feedback system.

These three metrics are well understood and highly measurable. They are important. Yet they are not enough.

They give very little insight into whether your product will meet your customer's *Eight Primary Values*. In fact, you could be performing very well on these three and be headed for disaster.

Very importantly, you must also measure the capability of your design to create waste and quality loss. That is why you must also measure your design's ability to minimize the seven root causes of poor quality and waste, the *Seven Evil Ings*.

Feedback Rule #2. Be cautious with metrics as the wrong ones can "kill" you.

Using a wrench to drive a nail can cause you a lot of pain. The same is true of design measurement tools. Too many design teams rush to use the wrong metrics, at the wrong time and in the wrong way.

Never rely on only one metric. For instance, I continue to encounter design teams that rate the quality of their new product based on design-for-assembly or manufacturability metrics.

Only later do many of them realize that DFM&A was not the major competitive issue.

Many of us continually encounter products that excel at manufacturability but miserably fail the test of marketability or even usability.

Feedback Rule #3. Use both "hard" and "soft" measurement.

The most important characteristic of a good set of metrics for customer satisfaction is to have a mix of hard and soft measures. In his book *Keeping Score: Using the Right Metrics to Drive World-Class Performance,* Mark Graham Brown emphasizes the importance of "soft metrics."

> *Soft measures are measures of customer opinions, perceptions and feelings. These are leading-edge indicators that should be used to try and predict customer behavior. The opinions and feeling of customers are extremely important.*

At the same time soft metrics have to be supplemented with hard measures of customer satisfaction. These are measures of what customers in the end do, not just what they say.

Examples of these are: gains and losses of customers, market share relative to competitors, and amount of repeat business.

I still meet participants in my design workshops that believe that some things cannot be measured. Don't ever believe this. Everything you will encounter in your product design world is measurable.

For example, one of the most important factors for an American male in purchasing a car is *imageability.* The car must convey the image his ego wants to project.

All car manufacturers today have both sophisticated and common sense techniques to measure such "soft" attributes.

Feedback Rule #4. Measure for direction first, precision later.

Improvement is a relative term. It is defined by a starting point, a goal, and a way of tracking progress from start to finish.

The first objective is to make sure your entire organization is heading for the same destination or goal. Or in other words, that it is heading north rather than south. Precision is not important at the beginning. Direction is.

Don't be afraid to use Delphi, or consensus measurement, to keep you on track. The word Delphi comes from the ancient Greek city of the same name. Lacking any form of scientific method, the city fathers there would gather round to share their collective knowledge and opinions.

There are some *Ilities* that are difficult to measure. The collective judgment of your team is far better than not having any measurement at all.

With the exception of your product's technical performance, very little about your design in its early stages can be measured with any degree of accuracy. But this does not mean you should not measure.

Feedback Rule #5. Get information on *Ilities* and *Ings* concurrently.

Don't make the mistake of optimizing one *Ility* or *Ing* at the expense of another. Take a *systems approach,* optimizing the total product and not just one success factor.

Use "spider" or "radar" charts to rate all *Ilities* and *Ings* concurrently. All metrics are shown on the same chart at the same time.

The *Lean Design Solution* scorecard technique you will learn in Chapter Six begins by having you baseline the existing product against the Eight Primary Customer Values.

A scale of 1-10 is used with a "10" being "world class excellence."

The existing product's waste is baselined by using an *Evil Ing* spider chart. Low waste is indicated by a "1." Extremely waste can be as high as a "10."

Using these two *Ility and Ing* spider charts enables you to see at a glance where your product needs the most work.

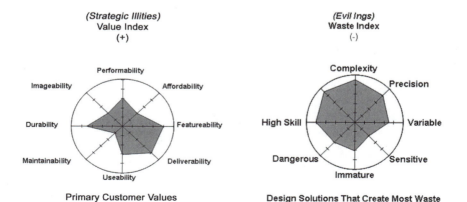

(Strategic Ilities) Value Index (+) — Primary Customer Values

(Evil Ings) Waste Index (-) — Design Solutions That Create Most Waste

Feedback Rule #6. Make sure everyone (especially management) is using the same feedback system.

Make sure your entire team buys into your measurement system and goals *before* you begin using them. The first goal of your measurement creation process is to help your team understand and agree on what problems must be solved.

Make sure your entire team agrees on the problems before you ask them to begin solving them.

Feedback Rule #7. Enable those who will be measured to create the measurement system.

Those who have the greatest responsibility for acting on the feedback should have the greatest say in creating the system that provides it.

When product delivery teams create their own measurement systems they will both "own" and use the measurements. Ownership is a powerful way to assure that a feedback system will be used.

The team then takes its goals and measurement system to management for their understanding — and approval.

In this chapter we have discussed the *Five Laws* that govern your success in solving your *Lean Design Equation.* However you and your team must have a way to integrate all of them into a powerful product design strategy.

This technique is called *Lean Design Mapping* and is the subject of the next chapter.

Lean Design Solution Tool

Tool Name: *Ility Value Baseline Tool*

Purpose: Use the *Eight Primary Customer Ility Values* as a way to understand how well you are performing with the "as is" product

Steps: 1. Each stakeholder gives his perception of how well the existing product is delivering each *Strategic Ility Value.*

2. A scale of 1-10 is used with a "10" indicating world class standard of performance.

3. Stakeholder must give his reasons "why" for the rating

4. These assessments are then used to begin understanding the starting point for the product improvement effort.

Primary Values Rating Tool	Rating	Why?
Performability (Example)	5	Our performance equal to, no better than our largest competitor. We have no points of differentiation.
Affordability		
Featureability		
Deliverability		
Usability		
Maintainability		
Durability		
Imageability		

Rating Scale: 1-2 Very Low 3-4 Low 5-6 Average 7-8 Good 9-10 Excellent

Section Summary

- You can only improve what you can measure.
- Real time feedback gives us time to make course corrections.
- Getting feedback on how we are improving product values (*Strategic Ilities*) and minimizing potential waste (*Evil Ings*) is essential for solving the *Lean Design Equation.*
- Both "hard" and "soft" metrics must be used.
- Product design measurement is extremely difficult at the early product concept stage. We must use *predictive feedback*, the use of metrics that forecast that a certain cause and effect relationship will take place in the sometimes distant future.
- Measure for direction first, precision later.
- Those who are to be measured should play a major role in creating the measurement system.

Chapter 3

Lean Design Strategy Mapping

Strategic thinking is the bridge that links where you are now to where you want to go.

Building that thought bridge must be your lean team's first order of business.

Strategic thinking is big picture thinking. It is "seeing the whole" before working on the parts.

> You've got to think about the "big things" while you're doing small things, so that all the small things go in the right direction.
> — Alvin Toffler

It's is figuring out how to defeat your competitors before they defeat you.

In this chapter I will share with you a powerful technique called *Lean Design Mapping* or for short, *LDM*. It helps you create a product strategy that will deliver more value with far less waste.

LDM ties together the *Five Laws of Lean Design* to help you solve the universal lean design equation you learned earlier:

Optimize Strategic Ilities, Minimize Evil Ings

Lean Design Mapping gets everyone on the same bus and headed in the right direction. Without a clear strategy, folks sometimes get on different buses headed in opposite directions.

The goals of *Lean Design Mapping* are the same as *Value Stream Mapping (VSM)*. Both are focused on eliminating waste and creating more value.

The big difference is that *Lean Design Mapping* helps you <u>prevent</u> *such wasteful tasks from ever having to be corrected in the first place.*

LDM is fire prevention. *VSM* is fire-fighting. A good fire department does both.

Your team uses *LDM* during an intensive one to two day team workshop, called a *Lean Design Kaizan.*

This *kaizan* brings together all those stakeholders who will play a major role in making your new product a success. The intensity is similar to *kaizan* events used by lean manufacturing teams.

The results of this strategy *kaizan* are then presented to management for its input and approval.

Don't expect that all strategic issues can be resolved during this first *kaizan.* Experience shows, however, that you will be able to agree on 60 to 70 percent of your lean product strategy.

In this chapter, I will introduce *Lean Design Mapping* to you and explain why it is so successful.

Then in Chapter Five, "A Lean Design Kaizan Step-by-Step, "I will give you a detailed guide for conducting such an event.

Lean Design Mapping Benefits

The purpose of *Lean Design Mapping* is to:

- Get everybody on the same page
- Surface disconnects, hidden agendas, or misconceptions right away
- Clarify design boundaries and map out the product "solution space"
- Quickly identify both technical and political hurdles
- Focus your team on your product's strategic values, or *Ilities,* as well as identify wasteful *Ings* you must avoid
- Create a "real time" feedback measurement system

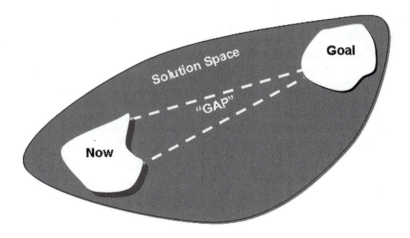

- Energize your team's innovative thinking get them into fast, meaningful action

Lean Design Mapping gives you a bridge to fill the "gap" between where you are now and where you want to be. It defines the solution space or dimensions of your design boundaries.

Today all product lifecycle issues must be considered "up front" at the early concept stage. That's the purpose of "integrated product development" (IPD). It's bringing back common sense to the design process.

While this notion of IPD is widely accepted and is delivering excellent results, too many product teams still struggle.

The reason: they are brought together as a team but are not given an adequate design road map to follow.

For example, manufacturing engineers are invited to sit in on lean design sessions to contribute their ideas. Many do.

But others, trained primarily to review completed designs, don't have a clear idea as to their role.

They are not given a model for their participation. And there is no clear way for them to contribute as the design evolves.

So many manufacturing engineers appear at the few first meetings and then fade away.

They only reappear again when the design is complete. And this may be too late for many changes to be even considered.

LDM Gives All Stakeholders a Product Design Role

Lean Design Mapping remedies this by giving each stakeholder a specific role throughout the entire product design process.

LDM uses techniques and tools that are easily understood. They can be used by everyone on an integrated product team.

Marketing, supply chain, manufacturing and even accountants can play an important role during the entire design process.

Very importantly, *Lean Design Mapping* gives Lean Champions, Black Belts, and project team leaders a step-by-step way to personally help a lean product design effort. It is an excellent tool for facilitators.

What is "Strategy" Anyway?

Lean Design Mapping takes the "fuzziness" out of the "front end" stage of your lean design effort. It's based on *strategic thinking*.

Strategic thinking helps you get a clear view of the entire forest before you go to work on the trees.

Unfortunately, too many product teams skip this important *strategic thinking* step and rush on to what some call "the real work" of design implementation.

There are two steps in a creating a product design. The first is *developing* the overall strategy. This is done during what is called the *concept phase.*

The second is *implementing* that strategy with detailed design, testing, and prototyping.

Never put the cart before the horse. Always do the strategy development part first. The implementation part comes second.

Most of us know how to implement well and use time-test techniques such as project management. What we stumble on most is the strategy part that is supposed to send us down the right implementation path.

Studies show that many product designs fail because of faulty strategic thinking, not because of poor technical skill.

Many times design teams leap into action before really understanding the underlying challenges or exploring enough alternatives.

Lean Design Mapping gives you a way for doing this quickly and effectively.

Strategy is a Continuous Journey

Your product strategy gives you a clear product development direction. A strategy enables you to mobilize your resources and focus them on what is most important.

Unfortunately, no strategy — like all product designs — is ever perfect. Strategies are compromises. They involve trade-offs between time, resources, customer wants, your company's resources and much more.

In addition, the *Three Sharks of Change* — customers, technology and competitors — are also constantly attacking the viability of your product strategy.

The upshot is that your strategy must be constantly reviewed to test its validity.

That is why *Lean Design Mapping* can never be a one-time event.

You must use *LDM* to revisit your earlier strategic thinking to see if it is still valid.

You can then fine tune your strategy to bring it in line with new realities.

"Strategy" Versus "Tactics"

I often find folks are confused about the difference between *strategy* and *tactics.*

Both terms are used in *Lean Design Mapping.*

Strategy development is a high level planning process. Tactics are used to deliver the strategy.

A good product strategy guides us in deciding what tactics to use

Never leap to "tactics" without first building a coherent strategy.

What is a lean design tactic? A lean tactic is an idea for implementing one or more of your strategic values or *Ilities.*

As you recall, these are the customer and company *values* you want to imbed in your product design.

The best kinds of lean design tactics are the ones that can improve multiple *Ilities* at the same time.

A tactic typically is a single idea. A strategy is the combination of tactics.

Tactics usually occur in a short burst. A strategy unfolds over a period of time.

For example, *reducing part count* is a lean tactic for delivering better *affordability*.

Another lean tactic is to *reduce the number of tasks* needed to service a product for better *maintainability*.

Good tactics should have a competitive angle to them. They show your customer how your product or service is competitively different.

In the next chapter you will learn *The Eight Top Lean Design Tactics* most used in product design.

Strategy and Tactics are Military Terms

The terms used in strategy development come from the "art" of war. How they are used in war strategy gives an better understanding of what they mean.

Example: In the Pacific during WW II, the American strategy was to attack the Japanese homeland quickly.

One of the tactics used was to "island hop to Tokyo." The idea was to attack only the key Pacific islands held by the Japanese.

This would leave Japanese soldiers on the other Islands to "wither on the vine" and eventually surrender.

This "island hopping" tactic proved successful with a savings in lives on both sides. However, the tactic didn't work completely. Some Japanese soldiers still had not surrendered as many as 25 years after the war.

Another example: In Europe, the Allied strategy was to crush Germany's ability to manufacture military equipment.

One major tactic was to bomb power plants and power generating dams. The British developed their famous "bouncing ball" skipping bombs to do this.

Another tactic was to destroy the ball bearing plants at Schweinfurt. Bearings are a key component in all military equipment.

This strategy failed. The Germans kept *increasing* their productive ability to make military equipment right up to the very end of the war.

Backwards from the Future Thinking

Lean Design Mapping uses the *Backwards from the Future* thinking paradigm I described earlier.

The analogy we use is that of climbing a mountain.

Lean Design Mapping "Mountain Model"

The example used is Mt. Everest. Every spring dozens of international teams attempt to climb this formidable peak.

No climbing team ever attempts to climb Mt. Everest without a clear strategy and a set of tactics to deliver that strategy.

Climbing teams never begins their strategic thinking at the bottom of the mountain.

They begin at the top.

They first mentally explore *when* they want to reach the summit. Timing is extremely important on Mt. Everest.

Only a narrow window of time is open for the climb to be made.

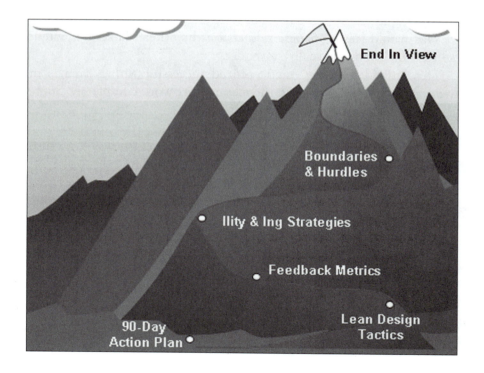

The team then mentally works their way down the mountain surveying obstacles, developing an overall strategy, setting up alternate schedules, innovating tactics and then developing a first cut action plan.

This is exactly how *Lean Design Mapping* works.

The mountain climbing team then iterates this process of thinking "top down" over and over again until they are convinced they have the safest, most successful strategy.

No two teams ever use the exact same strategy or the same tactics. There are many different paths to the top. There is no one "right way."

However, there is a right pattern of strategic thinking to follow. And there a few fundamental rules to know.

Lean Design Mapping can be used to climb a mountain or design a product. The benefits are:

1. Makes sure everyone is climbing the same mountain. The destination is clear right from the start, even though the path for getting there may not be.

2. Formalizes team tasks. Your team has a way to systematically work together right from the start.

3. Externalizes thinking. Team members have the opportunity to get their thoughts out on the table right away. Everybody participates right from the start.

4. Integrates knowledge. *Lean Design Mapping* encourages the sharing of knowledge and experience across all stakeholder disciplines.

5. Enables decision making. *Lean Design Mapping* gives you a format for making decisions, when appropriate.

6. Builds "common ground." Gets your entire team "roped together" with a common destiny and all heading in the right direction.

Lean Design Mapping enables you to quickly develop the first draft of your team's lean product strategy. It energizes your team for fast action.

It is a series of six steps. All of the steps are time driven. The team is given very specific tasks to do with clear deliverables at the end of each task.

Here, is a quick, thumbnail overview of the "What and Why" of *Lean Design Mapping*. A complete team facilitation guide is in Chapter Five.

Lean Design Mapping Step-By-Step

Step #1 – End-In-View

What? Team begins to agree on the overall "What, Why and When" of the design project, but not the "How." (The "How" is addressed later in Step #4.)

Misunderstandings, unanswered questions, and concerns are posted in a "parking lot" with an "owner" clearly named. While some can be answered immediately, the tough ones are revisited later.

Why? Orients the team toward the "destination," surfaces the reasons for the project and frames the timeliness of the task.

Benefit: This "End-In-View" task is the first step in bridging the gap between where you are now and where you want to go.

It begins to clarify your team's ultimate destination.

Lean Design Mapping uses a "future to the present" approach. The analogy is climbing a mountain backwards. You begin at the summit and then (in your imagination) *work down* the mountain through a series of steps.

You explore the best path to the top before you ever begin to climb the mountain.

Step #2 – Boundaries and Hurdles

What? Team identifies their "solution space," or the size of their "playing field." They then surface all hurdles they think they will face in reaching their "End-In-View."

This includes both technical and political hurdles.

The team uses the techniques of the *Law of Marketplace Pull* to understand where the *Three Sharks of Change* — customer, technology and competitor — are now and where they might go in the future.

Why? Expose misconceptions about design boundaries. Define hurdles so that they can be dealt with and overcome early. Reveal the competitive playing field.

Benefits: Prevents premature "duck diving." This is rushing to stick your head down into the weeds of detail without first knowing the "big picture." This step gives everyone the big picture so that they stay within the design boundaries in their thinking and action.

It also minimizes *shooting from the hip.*

This step defines the "solution space" of your new product effort. Backtracking is avoided. It also shows who are the major players in that solution space.

You always want to make sure your team is not making any false assumptions about where they can go or what they can or can't do.

You will find that many design teams reduce their design solution space. This is a natural tendency as tighter design boundaries can make finding solutions easier.

Step #3 – *Ility* and *Ing* Strategies

What? Using the *Eight Primary Customer Values* as a beginning checklist, the team agrees on the six to eight values, or *Ilities,* that will delight customers and satisfy your company. The team does this by applying the techniques of the *Law of Strategic Value.*

They then use the *Seven Evil Ings* as a beginning template for identifying the root cause drives of cost and poor quality. Your existing product is used as the baseline. All stakeholders contribute the worst examples for each of the *Seven Evil Ings.*

> The uncreative mind can spot wrong answers, but it takes a creative mind to spot wrong questions.
> — Anthony Jay

The team does this by using the techniques called out in the *Law of Waste Prevention.*

Why? Focuses the team on the customer values they must deliver to be successful. Helps them differentiate their product from the competition and begin to search for urgent customer needs.

The *Seven Evil Ings* analysis helps the team focus on the major waste creating design elements.

Benefits: Prompts your team to ask the right questions.

This step gets your team asking the right questions they need to answer to deliver a winning product.

They go *problem seeking* instead of the usual tendency to jump to *problem solving.*

Lean Design Mapping takes complex issues and long-term objectives, which can be very difficult to address, and breaks them down into manageable "chunks of value."

These can then be better understood and solved more quickly.

Example: If *serviceability* is a key value, you can begin defining what that means in the customer's mind and for his particular application. Creating an *Ility* strategy sets the direction of the design effort without undue constraints.

The "how to" of delivering these six to eight strategic values comes later during Step #5 of the *Lean Design Mapping* process.

Step #4 – Feedback Metrics

What? The team applies the *Law of Fast Feedback* to design their product measurement system. The team baselines the *"as is"* of their current (or competitor's) product.

They use the *Strategic Ilities* and *Evil Ings* identified in Step #3 above to do this task.

Each team member assigns a quantitative rating on a scale of 1-10. Most important, however, they explain the *why* of their rating. They will then use this same process to rate new designs as they are developed by the team.

Why? This task surfaces the individual views of each stakeholder. This enables the design team to see the "big picture." They more fully understand where they are starting from and the dimensions of the task they face.

> Strategy is first trying to understand where you sit in today's world.
> — Jack Welch, former Chairman of General Electric

Lean Design Mapping shows a design team how to quickly create a measurement system. This enables them to make "trade off" decisions between design alternatives.

Benefits: Calibrates team and then later, during their post-*kaizan* report out, calibrates management to the difficulties of the task as well.

Good strategic thinking says that you must first know where you are now before you start your design effort.

This step gives It gives the team a clearer idea of the *"as is"* before it tries to achieve the *"to be."*

Step #5 – Lean DesignTactics

What? Using the techniques of the *Law of Innovation Flow* as a guide, the team systematically brainstorms tactics for delivering each *Ility*. They do the same for generating ideas for preventing each *Ing*.

During Steps #1-4, the team was *defining* their lean design equation of *Optimizing Strategic Ilities, Minimizing Evil Ings*.

With this step they begin *solving* their lean design equation.

Why? This task is only the start of the team's innovation process. It gets existing solutions "out on the table." It gives the team an opportunity to flex their creative muscle.

> We tend to think of great thinkers and innovators as soloists, but the truth is that the greatest innovative thinking doesn't occur in a vacuum.
> — John C. Maxwell

Benefits: Team members can evaluate their solutions against the team's *Ility and Ing* strategy. A team member can quickly see if his favorite design idea is truly aligned with project goals.

Management can also see the beginning of the breadth and depth of the team's innovative thinking in solving their lean design equation.

Step #6 – 90-Day Action Plan

What? Team agrees on a "What, Who, When" action plan for the next 90 days. They also review open issues that were not answered or resolved during the *kaizan*.

These are assigned to individual team members for resolution.

Why? Gives team members a sense of accomplishment and enables division of responsibility. This step overcomes inertia. It "jump starts" the strategy delivery process. It also begins to test the validity of the team's lean design strategy.

The 90-Day Action Plan gives an opportunity for some "early wins."

Benefits: The tasks of delivering "chunks" of the product strategy can be divided among team members. Each of the six to eight *Strategic Ilities* can be assigned to an "owner."

This step helps the team sub-divide work without losing alignment with the End-in-View goal. Individual work can be done without the danger of design sub-optimization.

Management Report — Lean Design Mapping presentation

What? Team delivers a *Lean Design Mapping* brief to their management team immediately following their *kaizan*. This is a 60 to 90 minute presentation. It is supported with 10 to 12 power point slides.

The team uses the six steps as the outline of their presentation. This walks management though the logic used in crafting their lean design strategy.

Management is requested to hold questions until the team presents all six steps of the *Lean Design Mapping* effort. The floor is then opened for questions, comments and discussion.

The team leader then asks management to approve their 90-Day Action Plan, with any modifications made during the meeting taken into consideration.

Why? This presentation gives management an opportunity to see if your strategy aligns with the company's overall strategy. It surfaces any "disconnects" or disagreements between managers with regard to your project's objectives.

Benefits: Clearly shows management your team is thinking strategically. This step builds stronger management buy-in. It enables management to be a part of the design process without dominating it.

This makes management part of the solution, rather than later part of the problem.

> Three successive pursuits of the 80 percent solution produce the 99.2 percent solution. Pursuit of the 99 percent solution on the first attempt is a very poor investment of resources. All you have to get right on the first attempt are the fundamentals."
> — Maurice "Mo" Gauthier, US Navy Captain (Ret.)

The presentation shows management you are heading down the right path.

Lean Design Mapping an Iterative Process

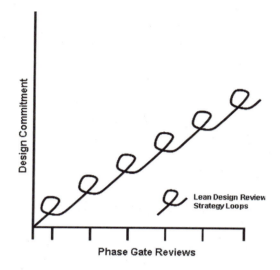

Strategies have a short shelf life.

Your lean design strategy must be seen as an active, explicit process. Product design development strategies degrade quickly.

The attack of the *Three Sharks* is relentless.

Your strategy only has value if it serves as a guide to action. It is worthless if it does not quickly and clearly communicate the objectives of your design effort.

That is why you must review your lean design strategy as you move through the product development phases. You must assure yourself that it is still valid in a rapidly changing world.

Reviewing your initial strategy will enable to quickly recalibrate your design direction, should that be needed. It will also re-energize your team.

Integrates Design Improvement Tools

There is no conflict between the use of *Lean Design Mapping* and any of your existing design tools, methods or techniques.

It is not a substitute for the rigor of a stage-by-stage product review process. Nor does it conflict with goals of *Design for Six Sigma*.

The output of your *Value Stream Mapping (VSM)* effort can be used as an integral part of the *Lean Design Mapping* kaizan.

Using *LDM* does not preclude the need for design tools such as Quality Function Deployment (QFD), Design of Experiments (DOE), Design for Manufacturability (DFM) or others.

What *LDM* does do is to help your design team decide which of these tools should be used and why and when. It helps you avoid using one of these tools in the wrong way and at the wrong time.

Lean Design Mapping acts as a framework for integrating your existing product improvement tools. Here are just some examples:

Design Tools

Design for Six Sigma (DFSS)
How Lean Design Solution Integrates Tool: Evil Ings create framework for attacking processes that create poor quality
Book chapter: Chap. 4. Design tactics for preventing poor quality from taking root

Quality Function Deployment (QFD)
How Lean Design Solution Integrates Tool: The Eight Primary Customer *Ilities* identify best values to deploy
Book chapter: Chap. 4. Techniques for creating your *Ility Value* strategy

Voice of the Customer (VOC)
How Lean Design Solution Integrates Tool: Ility and Ing Equation gives framework for VOC in three time dimensions
Book chapter: Chap. 2. *Law of Marketplace Pull.* How to listen to the voice of the future customers

Value Stream Mapping (VSM)
How Lean Design Solution Integrates Tool: Lean Design Mapping acts as front end tool for more detailed VSM
Book chapter: Chap. 5. *Lean Design Mapping Kaizan.* How to design a team design process

Design for Manufacture and Assembly (DFMA)
How Lean Design Solution Integrates Tool: Seven Essential Lean Design Skills gives basics for DFMA improvement
Book chapter: Chap. 4. Gives "how to" of parts and process reduction, product architecture simplification

Phase/Toll Gate Reviews

How Lean Design Solution Integrates Tool: Lean Strategy Thinking enables "seeing the whole before the parts"

Book chapter: Chap. 3. How to create an effective end-to-end product delivery strategy

Set-Based Concurrent Engineering

How Lean Design Solution Integrates Tool: Law of Fast Feedback a way to quickly evaluate many designs

Book chapter: Chap. 6. How to create *Lean Design Scorecards* and metrics

Summary

- Developing a lean product strategy is how you figure out how to beat your competitor before he beats you.
- Strategic thinking is imagining the desired future state and then using your thought process to work back from it.
- Designing your product strategy is a journey that never ends. It is not a destination. This is because the *Three Sharks of Change* are always reshuffling the deck.
- Strategy gets the big ideas all sorted out so that the small ideas can all be heading in the right direction.
- *Lean Design Mapping* guides you in creating the first draft of your team's overall game plan.
- *Lean Design Mapping* shows you when and how to integrate your existing design tools.
- All product strategies degrade and must be revisited in order to check their validity.

Chapter 4

The Seven Essential Lean Design Skills

Over the years I have had the pleasure of observing thousands of design teams in action.

I now know that the best teams have the ability to apply seven basic lean design skills. These seven skills are the bedrock of good lean design.

I am now firmly convinced that all lean team members, no matter the function they represent, should understand and be able to practice these *Seven Lean Design Skills*.

These *Seven Skills* enable you to:

Get the Ility Value Brothers Working For You

You were briefly introduced to these good guys when I explained the *Law of Strategic Value* Chapter Two. In this chapter you will learn ways to skillfully use them.

They are a valuable resource for helping your team find the right values that will differentiate your product, delight your customer and defeat your competitors.

Attack the *Evil Ing* Gremlins

You learned about these bad guys when I covered the *Law of Waste Prevention*. They are the primary source of all high cost and poor quality.

They are constantly waging a battle against the *Ility Value Brothers* for design dominance. You will never be able to completely defeat them. But you can minimize the pain they create. In this chapter you will learn skills for doing this.

Practice Systematic Innovation

This is the skill of knowing how to use the *Five Lean Targets* as a framework for finding new innovations.

You first learned about these when I discussed the *Law of Innovation Flow*. Now you will learn more tactics and techniques for systematically searching for new ideas.

Simplify Product Architecture

This is the skill of knowing how to build the right framework for integrating your product's functions.

A weak product architecture can be a major stumbling block that can stand in the way of improving your design over time.

Modularize if it Makes Sense

Modularity can help your team deliver a lot of *Ilities*, ranging from *manufacturability* to *maintainability* to *upgradeability*. If skillfully done, it can help you create a stream of new product benefits with a minimum of redesign.

However, modular design has to be done with the right strategic thinking in mind.

Minimize Parts and Processes

Fewer parts do not necessarily make a better product, but it is a good place to start. Part reduction is done by using a technique I call "functional implosion."

Parts are the embodiment of processes. Fewer processes means less cost and better quality. Six Sigma design is based on process simplicity.

The skill of process complexity reduction is one of the toughest to do well. In this section you will learn both skills of part and process reduction.

Simplify Assembly and Disassembly

Assembly is the final, very critical phase in the creation of any product. It is where major quality problems can occur. Skillful design teams know how to improve assembly without compromising disassembly required for servicing or disposal.

Applying these seven skills will simultaneously help you reduce cost and improve quality.

They will help get you on the right track in finding values that will "delight and differentiate" you in the eyes of your customers.

A Caution: Always remember, though, there is no "black and white" about any of these skills.

Each must be used with judgment and a good deal of common sense.

Rule of the Itch: Find your customer's most urgent itch and scratch it. You will then be at the head of the line for all future itches that emerge.

Skill #1 – Hire the *Ility* Value Brothers

You briefly met the good *Ility Value Brothers* in Chapter 1. These are the fellows who can help you find the Eight Primary Values all customers seek.

Now you will meet these guys one-by-one. You will learn how to use their combined "abilities" to solve your *Lean Product Equation.*

Get The Ility Value Brothers Working For You!

Maintainability

Affordability

Imageability

Durability

Performability

Deliverability

Featureability   Useability

Knowing the *Ility Brothers* well can also alert you to potential threats.

Competitors always seek to challenge your present product line by delivering more benefit along one — or more — of the *Eight Primary Customer Ility Value* pathways.

You must guard against your competitors using your weakness in any of these eight values as a way to gain dominance over your product line.

Begin by using the *Ility Brothers* as a checklist for seeing how well your current product is delivering value.

And listen to them as they guide you to finding the specific values your customers want.

As I describe each of them, I will share with you an example of how a successful company has enlisted the *Ility Brothers* to their advantage.

Brother Performability

This is the most overworked member of the *Ility Brothers* clan.

Performability stands at the top of your customer value list.

Performance is, of course, what customers look for first. Once assured *Brother Performability* is doing his job well, customers then seek other values.

Brother Performability has the key that opens the customer's door. He delivers the price of admission. He enables you to cross the threshold into the customer's domain.

Listen to this good fellow closely. He will clearly tell you what are your customer's real *needs* Not merely his *wants*.

Needs are far more powerful than *wants*.

Especially listen closely to *Brother Performability* when he starts talking about the most powerful kind of customer value: An urgent need.

Also listen to him closely when he starts talking about the future. When you do, he will help you predict what your customer needs will be in the future.

Brother Performability will also caution you against giving your customers more performance than they really need. This just adds up to wasteful cost and complexity.

This wasteful practice, called overshooting, can be just as bad as its opposite, undershooting. Undershooting is delivering performance below your customer's expectations.

Many times *Brother Performability* will make a suggestion that will deliver far greater performance at minimum cost.

Take for example, his advice to Heinz Catsup. Folks were always struggling to get the catsup out of the narrow neck bottle.

He suggested a 180 degree solution. Turn the bottle upside down to have the cap at the bottom, reverse the label and let gravity do the work.

Heinz listened and the rest is history.

Brother Performability's Characteristics

Typical Key Success Factors: Reliability, Quality, Performance meets or exceeds specifications
Good Performability: Airplane jet engines
Not So Good: Some commercial software
Examples of Metrics: Speed, fuel efficiency, computer memory
Worst Enemy: Complexity Gremlin who is always encouraging more performance than is really needed.

Examples

Classic Case Study: Black & Decker home power tools
Design Tactics: Adapted professional power hand tool design to home owner needs, lowered product life to reduce cost from $200 to roughly $50 or less, integrated parts and processes with engineered plastics

Questions Brother Performability will ask you:

- Can you reduce performance to lower cost and reach an entirely new market segment? (example: Shorter life power tool motors for less demanding home market)

- Can you integrate a new function that your competition has not thought of yet? (example: Design a power tool to serve as both a drill and a saw)
- Can you standardize components to help both the customer and our factory? (example: Same battery pack for all home power tools)

Brother Affordability

At first, *Brother Affordability* may strike you as a very stingy fellow. He is a Scotsman who is given to wearing tams and such to demonstrate his penny pinching ways.

He is always urging you to reduce cost as much as your can.

However, in the end, *Brother Affordability* is a common sense guy. He realizes cost is relative to the value received. That's why he is always looking for ways to help you deliver your customer more value at less cost.

You will find that he will always advise not to be afraid to increase cost if you can deliver value the customer really needs. Customers initially resist any kind of cost increase until you can show them the value trade-off.

One of *Brother Affordability's* biggest successes was Xerox. It was he who helped Xerox dominate the early copier market. Xerox had conducted extensive customer research that showed few people would be willing to pay five cents for a plain-paper copy when they could get a Thermofax copy for a cent and a half.

Fortunately for Xerox, they listened to *Brother Affordability*, who advised that customers would see the value of plain paper copying. Xerox listened, ignored the market research findings, and went on to dominate the early copier market.

Brother Affordability's Characteristics

Typical Key Success Factors: First time cost, operating cost, maintenance cost

Good Affordability: Cost/value equation of personal computers
Not So Good: Some medical systems
Examples of Metrics: Cost per mile, mean time between failure
Worst Enemy: Immaturity Gremlin who is always urging the use of not fully tested technology

Examples

Classic Case Study: Henry Ford who dominated the fledgling automobile market with his Model T that delivered dependable value without all the *frills* of automobiles of that day.
Design Tactics: Ford's tactic of one chassis fits all, availability of any color *as long as it is black* (black dried quicker), standard sub-assemblies and components.

Questions Brother Affordability will ask you:

- Can you substitute new materials to reduce cost? (example: Use of engineered plastics for automotive components)
- Can you integrate parts to reduce manufacturing cost? (example: One part composite auto bumpers)
- Can you standardize components for lower manufacturing and customer use cost? (example: Standard battery dimensions for all automobiles)

Brother Featureability

This is the youngest of the eight *Ility Value Brothers.*

He is always trying to help you find features that will set you apart from your competitors.

Many times he will help you find a feature to design into your product that costs very little but can make a big difference in your customer's purchasing decision.

Such was the case when he suggested to Chrysler Corporation the idea of coffee cup holders for their automobiles. Some on Chrysler's technical staff scoffed at first.

But *Brother Featureability* won out in the end. Coffee cup holder design became a big selling feature. Some European car makers didn't adopt the idea for several years.

Brother Featureability went on later to suggest another winner: sun visors with illuminated mirrors on the reverse side.

From time to time, however, you may have to keep this brother in control. He is always urging you to add new features. You typically do not want to add a feature that your customer does not want and does not need.

Brother Featureability's Characteristics

Typical Key Success Factors: Range of options, customization
Good Featureability: Harley-Davidson's *bolt on* accessories
Not So Good: Television remote controls
Examples of Metrics: Number of features per product
Worst Enemy: Variability Gremlin who is always encouraging more features than are really wanted, thus creating highly variable product platforms

Examples

Classic Case Study: Fledgling General Motors, which gained the lead in the previously Ford-dominated automobile market with different colors, options, wider choice of body styles
General Motors Featureabilty Design Tactics: Choice of car color, list of options, many model choices.

Questions Brother Featureability will ask you:

- Can you add a new, low cost feature to differentiate yourself from the competition? (example: GM's use of color choice against Henry Ford's *basic black*)
- Can you standardize features to offer a more attractive package to customers? (example: Automotive manufacturers standardizing on feature packages)
- Can you separate features to reduce standard product cost? (example: Automotive manufacturers offering heavier suspensions and special trailer towing packages as an added option)

Brother Deliverability

This brother is fast on his feet.

He wants you to deliver your product precisely when it is needed. He is a strong advocate of Just-In-Time delivery.

Brother Deliverability is good at helping you see wasteful time in your material-to customer cycle. He is a strong believer in factory floor *Value Stream Mapping (VSM)* and its goal of squeezing out wasteful time.

Brother Deliverability believes in the saying, *Time is money!* He is always urging you to trim the fat of excessive time anywhere along your product value delivery chain.

Brother Deliverability first made a name for himself when he advised Ray Kroc, founder of the McDonald's hamburger empire, to add the value of speed to his hamburgers.

Fast food was born because of that suggestion.

Dell Computers is also very thankful to *Brother Deliverability*. It was he that suggested to Dell the idea of modular components and a well-oiled supply chain as critical elements in their manufacturing and marketing strategies.

Now deliverability is at the top of the Dell value list, as well as that of its competitors.

Brother Deliverability's Characteristics

Typical Key Success Factors: JIT-ability, customized configuration by dealer or user
Good Deliverability: Dell computers
Not So Good: Furniture industry
Examples of Metrics: Dock to door time, raw material to customer sale time.

Worst Enemy: Precision Gremlin who is always encouraging you to use more skill in the production or use of products, thus requiring more time and expertise.

Examples

Classic Case Study: McDonald's and Ray Kroc who created new fast food market based on speed of delivery.

McDonald's Deliverability Design Tactics: Added speed to the menu, standardized offering, simplified preparation process, automated preparation process to reduce skill, improve quality.

Questions Brother Deliverability will ask you:

- Can you reduce the complexity of your product to minimize the number of life cycle process steps and time needed to deliver its value? (example: McDonald's menu standardization in early days of its growth)
- Can you substitute something in your product offering that will increase your customer satisfaction, yet shorten preparation time? (example: McDonald's now offering pre-packaged *health smart* salads, other foods on its menu.)
- Can you re-use something in your product to reduce total life cycle time? (example: McDonald's use of recycled paper products for packaging, thus supporting the *green movement* yet still being able to use disposable packaging.)

Brother Usability

This congenial fellow helps you answer your customer's question:

Will I be able to easily install it and learn how to use it?

Brother Usability delights in burning instruction manuals. He is always telling you the ideal number of pages in an instruction manual is zero.

He wants you to make your product so simple to use that it is

plug and play. It was he who came up with the saying, *It's a no-brainer!*

But *Brother Usability* is a realist. He knows that achieving a no-brainer can take time. Taking a human skill and converting it into a mechanized process is no easy matter.

He was the guy who turned on George Eastman, founder of Kodak, to the idea of making photography easy. Up to that time, taking photos was the sole domain of the highly skilled professional or serious amateur.

Brother Usability urged George to turn that notion upside down and the Kodak Brownie was born. Family picnics have never been the same since.

Brother Usability's Characteristics

Typical Key Success Factors: No-Brainability, Installability, Learnability
Good Usability: Disposable snapshot cameras
Not So Good So Far: Home entertainment systems
Examples of Metrics: Time-to-Master, Installation Time, Installation Skill
Worst Enemy: Skill Gremlin who constantly urges that skill is good, whether it is really needed or not, in the manufacture or use of a product.

Examples

Classic Case Study: Kodak Brownie camera that revolutionized photography making it accessible for the American family.
Kodak's Usabilty Design Tactics" First *Point & Click* Brownie camera, photo film mail in photo processing, simple *sun at your back* instructions

Questions Brother Useability will ask you:

- Can you integrate product functions to simplify the user interface? (example: Auto adjusting digital cameras that compensate for light, distance,"red eye," etc.)
- Can you standardize functions to make them common with other similar products? (example: Consistent use of common industry-wide standards and terms for camera manufacturers.)

- Can you separate features to make your products more *user friendly?* (example: Camera manufacturers offering both *popular* and *professional* series.)

Brother Maintainability

This trustworthy fellow helps you answer your customer's challenge:

Will it be easy for me to keep your product in service?

Notice the cobwebs on his phone. *Brother Maintainability* believes the best kind of maintenance is no maintenance. He is the strongest advocate for *Design for Six Sigma Quality.*

When service is required, he says make it as simple as possible for either the service man or the user. *Brother Maintainability* is always urging self diagnostics, even remote diagnostics for highly technical systems.

He wants to make product failure more predictable.

Brother Maintainability will tell you the best of kind of maintenance tool is the human hand. He is a strong believer in easily accessible modular components to reduce repair time.

His work with television manufacturers has given us the maintenance free TV set. When your new TV fails, a rarity today, your only option is to return it for another — or dispose of it.

A TV set failure is a rarity today due to *Brother Maintainabilitys* advice. TVs are now built with quality *designed-in.* Quality by design is so good that in-process quality inspection is becoming a thing of the past.

Brother Maintainability's Characteristics

Typical Key Success Factors: Easy problem finding, Replaceability, Component affordability, Lego-ability

Best Examples: Standard television sets

Not So Good Yet: Small aircraft maintenance

Examples of Metrics: Time-to-Repair, Repair skill required, Complexity of tools required

Worst Enemy: Danger Gremlin who is continually suggesting the use of solutions that are a danger to the environment or human beings. The systems that are in place to keep these safe constantly need a lot of maintainability to assure they are not hazardous.

Examples

Classic Case Study: Dell, which modularized computers for easy upgrade and maintenance

Dell Maintainability Design Tactics: Modular, easy to remove and replace components, streamlined express mail return process, standardized return packaging.

Questions Brother Maintainabilty will ask you:

- Can you separate product components to make them easier to maintain? (example: Use of modularity in computer design for plug and play maintainabilty)
- Can you standardize component interfaces to enable faster replacement and upgrades? (example: Use of standard interfaces for batteries, hard drives, etc. in computer design)
- Can you reduce maintenance learning time by automating problem finding process? (example: Use of diagnostics in computer problem finding process)

Brother Durability

This is the toughest of all the *Ility Value Brothers.* He helps you design products that will stand up to the toughest abuse.

He may look tough but under *Brother Durability's* robust exterior beats a kind heart.

What he really is after is product design that makes the world easier for both the manufacturer and the user.

He is always encouraging you to use materials that can withstand abuse. He definitely is against moving parts and precision part interfaces.

But what really gets his goat is the use of design solutions that are highly sensitive to damage or disruption.

His work with the automotive industry has improved the durability of car paint finishes, although, he will admit, there is still a long way to go.

One of *Brother Durabilitys* greatest wins was the Timex watch. It was he who helped Timex reduce precision interfaces and reduce moving parts to come up with the most robust watch of its time.

And it was *Brother Durability* who coined the Timex slogan: *It can take a lickin' and keep on tickin'!*

Brother Durability's Characteristics

Typical Key Success Factors: Timex-ability, Design for Robustness Good
Example: John Deere Tractors
Not So Good So Far: Some kids' toys
Typical Metrics: Time-Between-Failure, Service frequency, Cost of repair
Worst Enemy: Sensitivity Gremlin who urges design solutions that can't stand the abuse of man or time

Examples

Classic Case Study: World War II American Jeep
Durability Design Tactics: Jeep's simplicity of fewer parts, less skill to operate, interchangeable parts

Questions Brother Durability will ask you:

- Can you eliminate moving parts? Moving parts are subject to breakdown and wear. (example: Jeep's raw simplification from its simple "rag top" to its bare instrument panel.)
- Can you reduce the number of sub-assemblies or components? Failures normally occur at the interfaces between components. (example: Jeep's total number of components far than typical automobile of its day.)

- Can you increase the robustness of high abuse parts? (example: Jeep's beefed up suspension enabled it to keep up with the toughest Army tracked vehicles.)

Brother Imageability

This sharp fellow is the star of the entire *Ility Brothers* clan.

He wants you to design your product so that it immediately conveys an image of quality and trust.

He always says: *You never get a second chance to make a first impression.*

Brother Imageability helps you develop products that become the standard for your industry or market.

These are products like Kleenex tissue, Fed Ex service, Kodak film and John Deere tractors. He wants you to *own your category.*

The ultimate position to be in, *Brother Imageability* will tell you, is to have your product name become a verb or have it used for an entire category of products, no matter the manufacturer.

This is the case when your wife says she has run out of Kleenex, even though that's not the brand she purchased.

Or when you ask someone to *Fed Ex* a package even though your office may use UPS at that time. Or when you think of farm or home tractors and the only brand that comes to mind is John Deere (runs like a Deere!)

This guy helps you create products that convey an image of quality and prestige.

Brother Imageability will tell you your product image is a precious gem that must be polished and protected constantly. Losing your good image is like losing your good family name. It is sometimes impossible to regain.

It is this good brother who constantly reminds you that your product name is the single thing that distinguishes you from a sea of competitors.

The average mind is deluged with brand names and words during a single day. The average person can consume eight to ten hours of television, radio, books, newspapers, and videos a day.

This translates into 40,000 words a day, 280,000 words a week and more than 14 million words a year.

Brother Imageability says you must be able to design your product so that its name becomes the standard of prestige and quality. It was he who advised Gillette razors to keep ahead of the *Three Sharks of Change* by rolling out a never ending line of improvements.

Every two to three years Gillette replaces its existing blade with a new idea. In my bathroom drawer I have an old Gillette two-bladed razor (Atra). In there is a shock absorbent razor (Sensor). There is a three bladed razor (Mach 3). And I just bought a new Mach 3 Turbo with three new Anti-Friction blades.

Brother Imageability is doing a great job for Gillette.

Brother Imageability's Characteristics

Typical Key Success Factors: Brand recognition, quality image, customer loyalty, frequency of repurchase
Good Example: GE aircraft engines
Not So Good Yet: Modular home builders
Typical Metrics: Share of market, brand recognition, quality awards won, customer repurchasing data
Worst Enemies: All of the *Seven Evil Ing Gremlins* but especially the *Danger Gremlin* who can quickly ruin any product's good reputation

Examples

Classic Case Study: Gillette razors
Imageability Design Tactics: Keeps focusing on owning the razor product category by continually upgrading the product to defeat competitors.

Questions Brother Imageability will ask you:

- Can you reduce the number of tasks your customer must perform to use your product? (example: Changing a razor blade in a Gillette razor)
- Can you reduce any danger in the use of your product? (example: Gillette's easy-to-use blade discarding and loading system)
- Can you add a feature that clearly differentiates you from your competitor? (example: Gillette's relentless search for new features ranging from product packaging to razor blade storage)

Constantly waging a war against these good *Ility Value Brothers* are the *Evil Ing Gremlins*. They are always looking for ways to defeat the *Ility Brothers* in their quest for leaner product designs.

That is why *Attacking the Evil Ing Gremlins* is the second skill your lean product team must master.

This is where we will now turn in the next section.

Skill #2 – Attack the *Evil Ing* Gremlins

The Eight Gremlins of Waste

I briefly touched on this evil gang in Chapter Two when I described the *Law of Waste Prevention*.

The *Eight Gremlins of Waste* are the root cause of most product problems. They create both direct and indirect cost.

If you let them, they will defeat all your efforts at trying to achieve Six Sigma quality.

The good news is that they can be attacked by using smarter design solutions. While you will never be able to

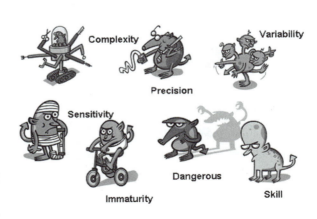

eliminate them entirely, you can minimize their impact by knowing how they work.

While the results of their efforts are first seen in the manufacturing domain, they continue their wasteful work all along your product's lifecycle path.

The lean manufacturing revolution is aimed squarely at reducing the waste that these gremlins cause on the factory floor. However, some of the worst pain they create appears later, in your customer's domain.

Members of this evil gang never work alone. Like any gang, they seek strength in numbers.

When you see one of these gremlins, you can bet a couple of more are close at hand.

Your entire design team must have both the skill to recognize these seven.

These seven gremlins provide a way for every team member to examine their area of expertise for potential waste.

They are used as a checklist for starting the important process of identifying and then eliminating waste.

Identifying where they lurk in your present products is the first step for focusing your lean design *waste prevention effort.*

Complexity Gremlin

The *Complexity Gremlin* is the leader of the *Evil Ing Gang.* He is the cause of endless, wasteful processes in all four product lifecycle domains.

His motto is *"More is better!"*

You can recognize his work by the number of different tools that are required to manufacture a product. Or the number of tools required to maintain a product.

The use of a complex design solution has a tremendous ripple effect that can turn into a tsunami wave of cost.

The wasteful *Ings* the *Complexity Gremlin* creates show up immediately in the design domain. And don't stop until the product's disposal.

In the *Design Domain*, complexity can add up to more engineering, prototyping, and testing.

In the *Supply Domain*, complexity can mean more suppliers with more costly components to manufacture.

In the *Factory Domain*, the *Complexity Gremlin's* work is especially noticeable. More complexity means more machines, people and non-value added process steps. Complexity also means more overhead cost.

The worst place to see product complexity is in the *Customer Domain*. Complex products unleash a whole string of non-value added tasks ranging from learning to maintaining to disposing.

Excessive product complexity can result in lost customers.

Good questions to ask about controlling the Complexity Gremlin:

- Can we *eliminate* some less important product *functions* to reduce complexity in the factory and customer use domains?
- Can we *reduce parts* to make the product less complex to design, supply and manufacture?
- Can we *re-use* previously designed parts and sub-assemblies to reduce the complexity of design, manufacture and service?

Precision Gremlin

The *Precision Gremlin* may look like a pleasant fellow when you first meet him.

But beware.

That calculator and fine scale ruler he always carries can create lots of headaches.

His motto is: *"The tighter the tolerance, the better!"*

The *Precision Gremlin* can create a trail of waste and poor quality. The best design is one that requires less precision, not more.

Excessive precision is evil. A precision process is one that demands that everything go right every time or the entire product can be flawed.

Minimize precision in all four product domains. I still encounter engineers that specify tight tolerances when a more open tolerance will suffice.

Precision is expensive in terms of machines, tooling, skilled employees and scrap. One way to start attacking precision is to review the tolerances now specified for your products and question whether they are really required.

Suppliers constantly point to excessively tight tolerances as a major source of high, non-value-added cost.

Good questions to ask for controlling the Precision Gremlin:

- Can we *standardize* how the customer interfaces with our product to minimize the need for precise steps to be completed in using the product?
- Can we *substitute* new materials for those that now require extreme precision in their manufacturing use?
- Can we *reduce* excessively tight tolerances?

Variability Gremlin

This multi-headed gremlin never knows which way to go. The only thing predictable about the *Variability Gremlin* is that he is always unpredictable.

The *Variability Gremlin* likes chaos. He is the guy that creates all those tough-to-control processes that are always getting out of control on your factory floor.

His motto is: *"Just do it!"*

Classic examples of his work are variable process steps like painting, coatings, and other multi-step processes. These require close monitoring to make sure all is going right. The cost of all this control is very

expensive, and if not done properly, can result in excessive scrap and re-work.

As Deming, the great quality guru once noted, the cure for a bad manufacturing process is ideally not his beloved Statistical Process Control (SPC), but the complete elimination of the troublesome process step or its simplification.

It takes skill and experience to control variability in a process.

I use the analogy of my mother-in-law's chili. No one has been able to duplicate her chili. This is despite the fact that every one of her daughters and daughters-in-law have carefully copied her recipe.

First there is the issue of the ingredients. There has to be just the right amount of meat, beans, tomatoes and spices. My mother-in-law was very careful in picking out these ingredients with her skilled eye.

Then there was the cooking of the meat. After simmering, the fat had to be drained but not all of it as this would have destroyed the natural flavor.

The tomatoes had to be sliced just to the right thickness. And then just the right amount of water must be added. Additional water must be added later as the chili continues to simmer.

Then there is the issue of cooking time. All of this requires a high level of process control and patience.

And since this entire chili making process is dependent on the skill and experience of the cook, the results can be highly variable.

I continue to see many cases on factory floors around the world where there is only one person who has the skill and experience to control a key process.

Good questions to ask about controlling the Variability Gremlin:

- Can we *separate* highly variable factory floor processes and *automate* them for better control?
- Can we *standardize* processes where humans are required to reduce the possibility of error?
- Can we *reuse* design solutions that have proven to be non-variable?

Sensitivity Gremlin

Whenever this guy is around things are always going wrong. He is the root cause of huge cost and quality problems.

Sometimes the *Sensitivity Gremlin* sometime can't be avoided. But try if you can.

When the *Sensitivity Gremlin* has done his work, you can have delicate parts that are easily flawed during factory or post-factory stages. These fragile items require special packaging, reworking and extra field service.

His motto is: *"Tough is too much trouble!"*

He has bedeviled auto manufacturers ever since they started building cars. The most sensitive part of a car subject to damage is its paint finish.

Millions of dollars are spent every year protecting, packaging, reworking and repairing paint finishes.

The finish on your car is also the most visible element of quality. It is the characteristic you see first.

No wonder automotive R&D departments are constantly seeking ways to make tougher paints and tougher finishes.

Good questions to ask about controlling the Sensitivity Gremlin:

- Can we *eliminate* a material or component that is highly sensitive to environmental damage?
- Can we *add* something that will toughen the sensitivity of the product?
- Can we *separate* manufacturing operations that are sensitive to disruption from those that are not so that we can better protect them?

Immaturity Gremlin

This diaper-clad fellow is the youngest member of the *Evil Ing Gang*.

You wouldn't think he could create much trouble. He just looks so innocent. But beware.

You've seen this guy many times before. He looks good on his shiny new tricycle. In fact you think he's going to put you head and shoul-

ders above your competition, but watch out! You could get you in trouble!

His motto is: *"New is always better!"*

The *Immaturity Gremlin* turns out to be the culprit when you try to use processes or technologies that are not quite proven for your application.

Even if the new technique doesn't prove to be an absolute failure, there is a high price to pay in learning curve time.

New technologies must be introduced with a good deal of care.

It was the *Immaturity Gremlin* that the plastics industry struggled with during its early days. Re-designing parts to be made of plastic rather than metal proved to be no easy task.

Using the same design to create a plastic part as was used for a metal one never worked out. It required a whole new way of design thinking.

A whole new science of plastics design had to evolve. All along the way the *Immaturity Gremlin* made his mark.

Good questions to ask about controlling the Immaturity Gremlin:

- Are we sure that *substituting* this new material will not create more problems than it solves?
- Can we *re-use* a design solution already proven in another industry?
- Can we *eliminate* the need to even use this new technology through the use of another design solution?

Dangerous Gremlin

Be on the alert for this guy.

The *Dangerous Gremlin* is always urging design solutions that create potentially hazardous conditions for the environment or we humans.

Dangerous solutions require non-value adding tasks such as training, certifying, inspecting, controlling and much more to make sure their potential danger doesn't ever happen.

Of course, we don't do this intentionally. It's just that we sometimes don't take enough care to understand the danger some design solutions can create.

The guy behind all of this is the *Dangerous Gremlin.*

His motto is: *"Don't worry about a thing!"*

The result of his work shows up in higher employee protection, disposal, liability, and documentation costs. All of this protection affects every company's bottom line.

The *Dangerous Gremlin* is especially well known to corporate lawyers. Entire legal staffs have worked for years trying to undo his handiwork.

Good questions to ask about controlling the Dangerous Gremlin:

- Can we completely *eliminate* the dangerous operation from our factory floor?
- Can we *reduce* the impact of a dangerous event happening with our product by designing in safeguards?
- Can we *substitute* a new process for the dangerous one?

Skill Gremlin

The *Skill Gremlin* is the most deceptive of all the *Seven Gremlins of Waste.*

Most folks think of skill as a good thing. But it really isn't when you tally up the cost of the customer — and your company — having to use it.

Skill is a human characteristic. Humans are fallible in the use of their skills. And highly skilled humans are most times hard to find.

The best approach is to minimize the amount and degree of skill needed to design, supply, manufacture and, again very importantly, use a product.

Take skill out of the entire product value chain. Only use it when you must.

You can always recognize the *Skill Gremlin* by his oversized cranium. He wants you to hire experts for everything.

While a certain expertise will always be needed, the practice of designing products that require a lot of skill is costly. It can also lead to a lot of quality problems.

An example from the *Manufacturing Domain* is the manual welding and soldering operations required for component assembly. These processes require skilled workers who must be trained, certified, and supervised, and their work inspected for quality.

In addition, human beings must also be motivated. Turnover rates can be high. Bottlenecks are common. Quality varies widely depending on which skilled worker is doing the job, and even the mood that worker is in.

Look for ways to squeeze skill out of your manufacturing processes through task simplification, open tolerances and, in some cases, automation.

Trying to quantify the real costs of operations requiring skill is tough. Much of this cost is buried in "hidden" overhead. It is not easily captured by conventional cost accounting procedures.

The U.S. Navy has been battling the *Skill Gremlin* for years. The Navy's Aircraft Carrier fleet is mounting a major campaign to reduce skill levels aboard ship. Their goal: Improve safety and mission effectiveness while reducing cost.

With this in mind, the Navy is now designing "smart ships" with extensive computerization and automation. The objective is to cut crew size, now standing at about 6,000, by half.

Another technique they are employing is crew training performed aboard ship, "on the job," instead of at costly on-shore facilities.

Good questions to ask about controlling the Skill Gremlin:

- Can we *standardize* tasks to make them easier to remember?
- Can we *automate* tasks to foolproof them?
- Can we *reduce* the number of tasks requiring skill to improve the odds against something going wrong?

Skill #3 – Apply Systematic Innovation

Peering up at me from my mouse pad is a photo of Thomas A. Edison, one of the most prolific inventors of all time. Above his white, bushy haired head is Edison's quotation:

"There is always a way to do it better…find it!"

This third Lean Design skill is all about *systematically* finding Thomas Edison's "better way." Here you will learn a new way to think about finding design solutions.

> Innovation success is more likely to result from the systematic pursuit of opportunities than from a flash of genius.
> — Peter Drucker

It will change the way you and your team look at a product. When you change the way you look at things, things change.

Albert Einstein also recognized the power of changing the way we see things. When asked what single event was most helpful to him in developing the theory of relativity, Einstein answered:

"Figuring out how to think about the problem."

Innovation is changing your perspective. Innovation can be as simple as looking at something from a different angle.

Take the ordinary paper clip, for example. Folks have been finding new uses for paper clips since it was invented over one hundred years ago.

And each year the U.S. Patent office sees new applications for different types of paper clips.

Henry Petroski in his book *The Evolution of Useful Things* (Vintage Books, 1992) recounts the results of research conducted by Howard Sufrin, heir to the Pittsburgh family business that made Steel City Gem Paper Clips.

Sufrin commissioned a study in 1958 to determine how paper clips were used.

He found that three of every ten paper clips were lost.

Only *one in ten* was ever used to hold papers together.

Other uses included:

- toothpicks
- fingernail cleaners
- ear cleaners
- makeshift fasteners
- tie clasps
- chips in card games
- markers in children's games
- decorative chains
- weapons

Paper clips have been used as political statements.

Norwegian citizens during World War II fastened paper clips to their jacket lapels to show patriotism and irritate the occupying Germans.

Wearing a paper clip in Norway could result in arrest. The function of the paper clip, "to bind together," took on the symbolic meaning of "people joining against the forces of occupation."

Man's inventiveness when it comes to paper clips — and most everything else — seems endless.

We all want our organizations to be more innovative And to be able to do this not just on one or two projects but every day of the year.

Yet delivering consistent, outstanding innovative achievements remains an elusive goal.

Some companies manage to do it. Many companies do not.

Organizations, the marketing expert Theodore Levitt once noted, by their very nature are designed to promote order and routine.

They are inhospitable environments for innovation.

So busting out of the routine and orderliness of corporate life requires some serious changes in how we think about and see things.

A diversified lean product team with a good innovation process can turn such an inhospitable environment into a friendly one.

The reason? No two people ever see the world in exactly the same way. Diversity opens many paths to new ideas.

The *Lean Design Solution* uses a technique called *systematic innovation*. It is a way to *focus* your innovation energy where it counts most.

Research shows that folks are sometimes more creative when they must act within a focused, constrained framework.

In product design, focus and boundaries boost creativity.

Take brainstorming, for example. I am not a great believer in *random* brainstorming.

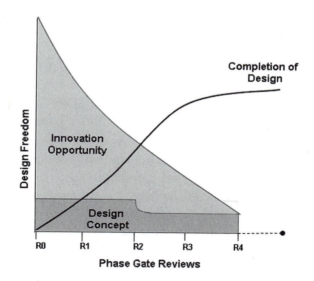

This is the collective effort of coming up new ideas, most of which are linked to one another as in a chain.

I find such random brainstorming to quickly lose focus. Many times such an effort goes quickly off track.

I am a great believer in *systematic* brainstorming. This is the practice of constraining your brainstorming effort and focusing it, like a laser, on what is critically important for your success.

The *Strategic Ilities*, the customer values that you have decided are most important, create the boundaries for focused innovation.

So do the *Evil Ings* and the wasteful examples you have identified as being the worst.

The *Ility and Ing Equation* brings focus and boundaries to your design effort, without the problem of too much constraint.

They are at a high enough level to give you plenty of solution space to search. Yet they are focused enough to keep you on the right track.

The Five Basic Product Elements

The *Lean Design Solution* gives you a way of applying the *Ility and Ing Equation* to the *Five Basic Product Elements*.

It then shows you eight ways for systematically thinking differently about each of these five primary elements.

I call these five product elements *targets* and the eight ways for changing them *tactics*.

The result is a new set of eyeglasses for seeing things differently.

The five primary elements of all products are:

- **Functions.** The *values* the product or service delivers across its entire lifecycle.
- **Parts.** The sub-assemblies or components that both individually and collectively *deliver the functions.*
- **Processes.** All the tasks required to deliver the functions. These tasks occur in the *four lifecycle domains* of design, supply, manufacture and customer use.
- **Materials.** The materials used to both create and operate the product throughout its lifecycle.
- **People.** All those folks who help deliver the functions, parts, processes and materials noted above.

Each of these *targets* offers plenty of room for innovative thinking.

Common Glass as Example

An engineer in one of my lean design certification workshops once used a glass to explain his definition of a "lean thinking" engineer:

An optimist looks at a glass and says the glass is half full.
A pessimist looks at the same glass and says it is half empty.
A lean thinking engineer looks at the glass and observes that it was designed twice as big as it needs to be!

To explain these five targets, I will use the glasses in our kitchen cabinets as an example.

Functions

The primary function of the glass is to hold liquid. But I have found it works equally as well for such functions as holding paper clips, coins or the pencils and pens on my desk at this very moment.

Many products are used for functions never thought of by the original design team.

Aircraft jet engines are used for breaking land speed records.

Latex-based paint was the liquid first used for White Out™ correction fluid.

Skin-So-Soft™ bath oil is now sold for mosquito protection.

Paper clips turn into tie clips.

All products can have multiple functions.

The same holds true for the *functions of the parts* that make up a product. All parts in a product have a minimum of two functions and sometimes many, many more.

This is quite clear for complex systems like jet engines. But it is also true for a single part product, like a glass.

The slightly tapered shape of the glass, or its uneven surface, can fulfill the function of you *holding it* more securely.

The surface of the glass can fulfill the function of advertising a product.

Identifying all potential functions of a product can lead to some innovative thinking for reducing the other four of the *Five Basic Lean Targets:* parts, processes, materials and people.

Functional Analysis

Try this: Systematically review the functionality of a part in your product. Use a *verb and noun* combination to describe its functions.

Remember: All parts have multiple functions. You may be amazed by some of the functions you overlooked. Or you may be startled by a new function — or benefit — you can add to your product without any additional cost.

Example: Think about the sun visor in your car. Its function years ago was simply to "block the sun." Count the functions it now serves today.

A good lean design technique is to reduce part count by combining functions of several parts into one part. By integrating functions into fewer parts, we can eliminate a whole plethora of possible problems down the line.

How to do this is described later in Skill #6, "Minimize Parts and Processes." This is when I describe the technique of *functional implosion.*

As you recall from the *Law of Innovation Flow* described in Chapter Two, functions exist in all three major levels of a product:

- system functions
- sub-system functions
- part functions

A common challenge is when a product takes on too many functions. Gadgets with such high complexity make them difficult to use.

They can also confuse the user. The *Complexity Gremlin* is hard at work in the American home.

Examples of this can be found in every household. Take a product as innocuous as a blender.

Let's be honest, we may use the "pulse" button every once in awhile, but for the most part "blend" seems to do everything you could want in a blender. Why there are 10 more buttons on the thing, I have yet to discover.

Some TV remotes nowadays look like they could fly the Space Shuttle. Some are so confusing that many find it easier to just get up and change the entertainment device manually.

With dozens of buttons that will operate a variety of devices, some would find it more convenient to have three remotes – one for the TV, one for the DVD, and one for the Surround Sound receiver.

Complexity Explosion

The opposite of functional implosion is *complexity explosion*. This is the failure to simplify a system through standardization, elimination and other lean design tactics I will discuss later.

The "system" of glasses in our kitchen is a perfect example. I did a survey and this is what I found:

- *More than half* of our upper cabinet space is used for storing glasses.
- There are over *25 different types* of glasses (this does not include mugs or coffee cups!).
- There are more than *175 glasses*, many of which have not been used in years.
- I only use two of these glass types.

My wife, like many homemakers, is always complaining about a lack of storage space. Following my survey, I proposed that we reduce the complexity of our system of glasses.

I never got off first base.

As you can guess, I am still fighting the "battle of the glasses". The natural condition of man, and woman, is in the direction of complexity.

Simplicity requires far more effort.

Parts

Parts are the second of the *Five Basic Product Elements.*

Parts are always favorite targets of design teams.

Why is that so? The reason is their *high visibility.*

Parts have a geometric shape. They are "real." They can be measured, weighed, and counted.

Take the manufacture of glasses for example. Some glasses in our kitchen have multiple parts such as the plastic multi-walled insulated tumblers with the advertising on the outside.

This plastic glass is complex compared when compared to the one-part clear juice glasses that have been kicking around in our household for many years.

Accounting for the *direct cost* of glasses is relatively easy. It is simply a matter of adding the cost of their material with the labor used to produce them. You can even smell and hear them being manufactured on a glass manufacturer's factory floor.

However, never be fooled into thinking that just reducing parts can get you a lower cost product. When you combine the functions of multiple parts into one part, the resulting component can be so complex that its cost is far higher than the individual parts.

Part complexity can drive high "hidden cost." In the *Design Domain,* such parts require more design time and validation. They also can be risky in terms of their performance.

You can tell the *High Skill Gremlin* has been around when you see parts that are tough to design.

In the *Supply and Manufacturing Domains,* part complexity can result in more expensive equipment and tooling.

In the *Customer Use domain* part complexity can mean more service part cost.

Lifecycle Processes

The most elusive of the *Five Basic Lean Targets* are a product's *lifecycle processes*. This third product target includes all the tasks, or *Ings*, that have to be done like *designing, testing, manufacturing, selling, installing, training, maintaining*, and *disposing* of a product.

Most of these are elusive because they are *hidden* from the view of you and your design team. It is difficult to attack something that you cannot see. It's much like shadow boxing.

Accountants especially have a difficult time showing us the cost of such *hidden Ings*. The *Ings* of "direct costs" are fairly easy to track. These are such things as *machining* and *assembling*.

It's the "indirect costs" such as *storing, repairing, moving* and many others that pose the problem for accountants and design teams alike. Accountants deal with these indirect *Ings* by lumping them together as "overhead."

Peanut Buttering

They then spread these (a process sometimes called *peanut buttering*) over many products to develop a *standard burden rate* for cost accounting purposes.

You can see the handiwork of the *Danger Gremlin* when you see overhead costs that come with using chemicals that require a lot of protecting, monitoring, documenting, disposing and more.

This helps keep the books straight and the accountants employed but doesn't tell the design team much about the "what" and "how" of reducing such indirect *Ings* through better design.

I used to struggle endlessly with company managers on the issue of addressing such hidden costs with better design. I would show them how the *Seven Gremlins of Waste* created such hidden *Ings*.

I would point out how their overhead costs were skyrocketing due to these hidden expenses. The advent of *activity based costing*, the practice of allocating overhead costs to specific parts and products helped a little.

But most times my arguments fell on deaf ears. Material and direct labor cost were used as the only measure of value for a cost reduction effort.

Only with the arrival of the lean manufacturing revolution did managers come to see the value of identifying and reducing such hidden costs. The targets of most lean manufacturing work are focused mainly at these *Evil Ings*.

The techniques of value mapping on the factory floor are doing the job the accountants were unable to do.

For a masterful explanation of why mass production cost accounting can drive bad decisions, see Bruce Henderson and Jorge Larco's *Lean Transformation* (Oklea Press, 2000)

Materials

Product materials, like parts, are highly visible and a clear target for lean designers. There is nothing fuzzy about something that can be measured precisely, both by weight and cost.

Shaving weight and cost off any product is always a first choice for design teams. The only problem is that too many times previous design teams have beat the lean team to the punch.

There is the opportunity to substitute a new material for an old one. The arrival of engineered plastics created a bonanza for plastics suppliers.

But like all material substitution strategies, it was fraught with problems.

Many design teams did not clearly understand the characteristics of the new materials and had little knowledge about how to design with them.

Rules for designing with plastics were slow in coming.

The primary rule with new materials is to be ever watchful for the *Immaturity Gremlin*.

People

I believe that people, all the folks who have to perform all the life cycle *Ings* a product design requires, are the most neglected of all the *Five Lean Targets*.

Take for example the glasses I described earlier. Glass manufacturing is now highly automated.

It is in the *Customer Use Domain* where people emerge as the real opportunity for improvement.

Glasses have to be safely packaged, shipped, unpacked, stocked on shelves, purchased, washed, used, washed and stored.

All of these *Ings* are highly people intensive.

Perhaps that is why the self stacking, disposal plastic cups are so prominent now on supermarket shelves.

The Eight Lean Design Tactics

There are eight basic tactics you can use to simplify the *Five Primary Product Targets* I described above.

These can be used in combination. One tactic can be used across all five targets. Or all eight can be used to simplify one target.

There are also many variants of each. However, all members of your lean design team must know the following basic eight:

- **Elimination** example: Eliminate a *function.*
- **Reduction** example: Reduce *lifecycle processes*
- **Substitution** example: Substitute a new *material*
- **Separation** example: Separate *people* from dangerous processes
- **Integration** example: Integrate *many parts* into *few parts*
- **Re-Use** example: Re-use a proven *manufacturing process*
- **Standardization** example: Standardize how *people* interface with the product
- **Addition** example: Add a *function* to improve customer value

Eliminate

Using the tactic of elimination can have a major simplicity "ripple effect." For example, eliminating a product function can results in fewer parts, processes, material and people.

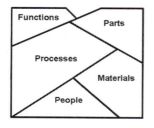

Can We **Eliminate** A Function?

Leaving something out in a new product can lower costs to the point where you may be able to tap an entirely new market.

Example: The first Volkswagens to arrive in America had far fewer functions and features than their American counterparts. Their cost was also much lower.

The result was to enable many used car buyers to be able to buy a new car. The tactic of functional elimination gave Volkswagen a foothold in America.

Eliminating a function can also force you to think how you can deliver the remaining functions more effectively. Such a design tactic helps *focus* your product design effort.

Reduce

You don't have to completely eliminate one of the *Five Lean Targets* in a product to have a major effect. You can simply *reduce* one of the five.

Take for example the case of Jet Blue, Song, Spirit and other point-to-point discount airlines. They have reduced the range of travel options for travelers and cut back on in-flight services.

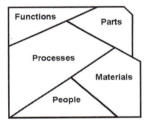

Can We **Reduce** Parts?

In so doing they have reduced the number of people required to run their airlines, as well as the cost.

They have changed the airline industry forever.

Substitute

The substitution tactic calls for questioning everything. Can the existing *material* be replaced with another that is less costly and easier to use?

Can a people process be replaced by an automated one?

Can a complicated *manufacturing process* be replaced with a simpler one?

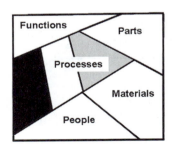

A good substitution thinking technique is to *ask why five times.* My Japanese partners taught me this trick. Every time I would explain why were making a certain design decision, they would ask another "why?"

Asking why five times forces you to get down to the very roots of your thinking. It opens up your mind to ideas that you never thought of before.

A classic example is the classic Heinz ketchup bottle. People would constantly complain about the difficulty of getting the ketchup out of the narrow necked bottle.

Heinz resisted any design change to the bottle. They saw the classic shape as a brand recognition feature. They also argued that the difficulty of getting the ketchup out pointed to its rich bodied taste.

The story goes that people continued to ask why? Heinz experimented with wider mouth bottles but it still was tough to get the ketchup out without a lot of vigorous shaking.

Folks continued to ask why it was tough to get the ketchup out from the bottom of the bottle.

Today you can buy Heinz ketchup with the bottle resting on the cap and the label reversed. Heinz practiced "180 degree" thinking and solved the problem.

Separate

Separation is the tactic of dividing any of the Five Product Elements into smaller "chunks" that can be easier to outsource, assemble and maintain in the field.

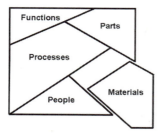

Can We Separate Materials?

A well known example is Dell Computers.

Dell has structured its computer architectures so that it can outsource all major components.

They have developed a product architecture that has clear lines of functional and interface separation. Functional sub-systems can be easily outsourced

The result is that they have less inventory to carry. They can also upgrade their computers "on the fly" with new or less costly components.

You will have a close look at how to do this kind of architectural separation in Skill #4 "Simplifying Product Architecture."

Dell customers also find it far easier to replace components for service.

Integrate

Integration is the design tactic of linking two — or more — of the *Five Lean Targets*.

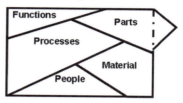

Can We **Integrate** Parts?

Parts can be integrated by combining their functions into one part.

Materials can be integrated by co-molding.

Insert molding can combine both metal and plastic parts.

Re-Use

Re-use is the practice of seeking previous design solutions for use in new design challenges.

One is the tactic of using previous part numbers in new product designs. There is nothing new to specify, outsource, manufacture or stock in a customer's inventory.

It can also mean the re-use of previous engineering solutions that are "tried and true." Re-use can minimize risk.

But you do have to be careful. Design solutions are *application specific*. You must make sure that the new application is similar, if not identical.

Re-use is also a good faster-time-to-market tactic. It minimizes the amount of testing required for a new process or part.

Microsoft is an expert at re-using software interfaces that their customers already know. Re-use reduces learning time. It also minimizes mistakes.

Standardize

Standardizing is the technique of designing products that use consistent, easily available components. It can also mean using standard user interfaces to reduce the time in learning how to use the product.

There are two types of standardization. *External* standardization is adherence to industry or government specifications. It can also mean using generally accepted processes for solving engineering problems.

Internal standardization is using company parts lists, specified suppliers and other guidelines. Like re-use, standardization minimizes risk

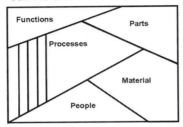

Can We **Standardize** Processes?

if the application in which the standard is applied is not significantly different than what it was originally specified for.

Where we get in trouble is when we attempt to use a standard solution for a special case.

Standardization does not deny you the opportunity to seek competitive victories. The small battery industry is a classic case of rigorous dimensional standardization.

Yet the small battery market is one of fierce competition. First there were the Eveready^{TM} zinc-carbon batteries. These were challenged by PR Mallory with their alkaline battery line called Duracell.^{TM}

Now lithium batteries are stealing a march on both.

One of the biggest practitioners now is the U.S. military. In days past, the military would require components to "mil specs." Now the move is to "cots" components that are "commercial off the shelf."

Add

The story is told that Guttenberg, the father of moveable type, was once walking along a country road when he spied a wine press. Earlier that day he had visited a coin factory.

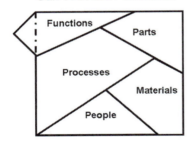

Can We **Add** Functions?

Suddenly he put the two concepts together and came up with the idea of moveable type that revolutionized the art of printing. This spurred the growth of knowledge and changed the way we looked at our world.

Sometimes the idea for adding something takes centuries.

In his digital book *How to Develop Winning New Product Ideas Systematically,* Roni Horowitz reminds us that ice cream was invented in about 2000 BC, but the edible ice cream cone was not invented until 3,900 years later.

Humans have been eating meat since the beginning of time and bread has been around for a few thousand years.

But the sandwich was invented only a few hundred years ago.

Discovering that adding something can bring value requires thinking differently.

Innovation Matrix

Following is a *Lean Design Solution Innovation Matrix*. Its purpose is to help your team *think* differently so that you can better solve your *Ility and Ing Equation.*

The *Innovation Matrix* arrays the *Five Product Targets* against the *Eight Lean Design Tactics.*

The object is to explore many solutions, no matter how extreme or crazy they may seem.

The only constraint is that they must be directionally correct with regard to your quest for maximizing your *Strategic Ilities* and minimizing your *Evil Ings.*

Lean Design Solution Tool: *Lean Targets/Tactics Matrix*

Targets/ Tactics	Functions	Parts	Life-Cycle Processes	Materials	People
Eliminate	Can we eliminate a function?	Can we eliminate any moving parts?	Can we eliminate any customer processes?	Can we eliminate any costly materials?	Can we eliminate the need for skilled people?
Reduce	Reduce functional performance?	Reduce parts by combining functions?	Reduce complex processes?	Reduce amount of material required?	Reduce number of people required for service?
Substitute	Substitute a new function for an old one?	Substitute an off-the-shelf part?	Substitute a known process for a new one?	Substitute a more easily manufactured material?	Substitute lower skilled people?
Separate	Separate functions to improve use?	Separate parts to make them easier to service?	Separate automated processes from manual ones?	Separate insert molded parts for easier re-cycling?	Separate dangerous materials from humans?
Integrate	Integrate functions to make it easier to use?	Integrate several parts into one multi-functional part?	Integrate several process steps into one?	Integrate two materials into one part ?	Integrate human tasks into automatic ones?
Re-Use	Re-use a previous functional solution?	Re-use previously proven design solutions?	Re-use conventional manufacturing processes?	Re-use well known materials for less risk?	Re-use same people for similar tasks for better quality?
Standardize	Specify a standard functional process?	Use standard, off-the-shelf high production parts?	Specify standard service processes?	Use readily available, low cost materials?	Design product for standard skills and techniques?
Add	Add a function to improve overall value?	Add parts to simplify repair?	Add processes to assure quality?	Add materials to deliver more performance?	Add people to provide better, faster service?

Skill #4 – Simplify Product Architecture

Your product's architecture is like the framework of a house. Once it's set in place, there is very little you can do to change it without a lot of cost and consternation.

Just ask anyone who has undertaken a major home remodeling job.

Your product's "architecture" determines how it will deliver the values your customer seeks.

It is the *art* of combining functions, parts, processes, materials and people to deliver the values your customer seeks at the maximum benefit for both you and the customer.

Product architecture impacts not only how your customer will *use* the product, but also the ease with which your suppliers and factory can *manufacture* the product.

Architectural strategy is one of the most important decisions to be made during your product design concept stage. Once in the marketplace, your product's architecture is very difficult to change without a significant impact on manufacturability and maintainability.

A *Lean Design Kaizan*, as described in Chapter Five, puts you on the right course for discovering the best architecture for your product.

Notice I use the word "art" in defining product architecture. There is no one "right" architecture for any given product. Many factors have to be considered.

What Is the Best "Product Architecture?"

Creating your product architecture is the task of transforming product functions into a physical form.

It is the first step in your *system level design*.

A product's architecture organizes product *functions into a framework*. For example, it is the challenge all architects face when designing a home.

The functions are such elements as cooking, eating, sleeping, entertaining and storage. The physical forms these functions take are kitchen, dining room, bedroom, family room and garage.

Creating your product architecture is a major decision in your product strategy. It directly impacts how well you are able to solve your *Ility and Ing Equation*.

Like everything else in product design, however, product architecture is a compromise among a combination of values.

Integrating Functions into Components

"Chunking" is the first step creating your product's architecture. This is the process of looking at ways to integrate functions into your product's physical components.

A "chunk" is a grouping of functions into one geometry. The word is used to define a system, sub-system or sub-assembly, or a part..

There are two types of product architectures: modular or "open" and integral or "closed."

In a modular architectural product strategy, product functions are imbedded in clear, well defined "chunks" or physical components. The interfaces between these components are simplified and, in some cases, designed to industry standards.

Clear, well-defined interfaces between these "chunks" makes it easier to upgrade a product. It also makes it easier to offer many variants without having to "reinvent the wheel" every time.

Outsourcing these chunks becomes relatively easy.

A negative is that modular architectures are relatively easy to copy. Product differentiation cannot rest on the outsourced components.

A good example of modularity carried to the extreme is the Dell computer on which I am writing this book. I chose it for its ease of component replacement.

When one fails, all I do is send it in and a new component arrives in the return express mail.

In an integral or closed product architecture, functional elements are integrated into one or very few chunks. This leads to fewer components, but with higher complexity in each component.

The interactions and interfaces among such integral components are complex. A change in one component can have a major impact on a number of other components.

Products with integral architectures can be difficult to outsource. This is because of the complex interaction of the components.

One benefit of an integral architecture is differentiation. Integral architectures are more difficult to copy.

A good example of an integral architecture is my home office Canon combination fax-copier-scanner. I bought it because it met my needs for space conservation and low functional usage.

A classic example is author David Cutherell's comparison of a Swiss Army knife with a kitchen carving knife (PDMA Handbook, 1996, p. 220)

The modular Swiss Army knife has multiple blades, each with its own function. One blade or tool can be used independent of another.

The integral kitchen meat carving knife has only one specialized blade. The blade and the handle are of integral construction. The knife is designed specifically for the household market.

Which Architecture Is Best?

Like design solutions, the architecture used is not black and white, but a strong shade of gray. Design strategies can be a combination of both.

Your decision as to which of the two architectures to use — modular or integral — is best seen through the lens of your strategic *Ility and Ing Equation.*

Following is a checklist using the *Eight Primary Customer Ilities* as the basis for comparison:

	Integral Architecture	Modular Architecture
Performability	Performance fixed yet can be more efficient	Performance can be altered due to ease of modular interfaces
Affordability	Can be lower in cost with one structure carrying many functions	Can be higher in cost due to the need for separate structures for "chunks"
Featureability	Relatively fixed at time of manufacture, difficult to upgrade	Architecture can be structured to carry a wide variety of features
Deliverability	Entire product must be kept in stock, not just main component	Component standardization can mean less inventory yet faster service
Usability	User interface can be specialized for one market	User interface typically the same for all customers
Maintainability	Product may require higher skill, more time for service	Enables easy replacement of wear items
Durability	Can be more durable due to fewer component interfaces	Many modular components mean more opportunities for failure
Imageability	Product can be customized for specific market	Modularity can bring "sameness" to product image

A Case of Functional Confusion

Home entertainment remote controls persist as the most notorious examples of product architecture. You would have thought they would have solved the problem by now.

Watching television should be one of the most relaxing experiences you can have in your home.

Take the example offered by Dr. Jakob Nielsen of the Nielsen Norman Group, a company that evaluates user interface designs. A *New York Times* reporter asked him to take a look at the remote controls he uses in his home.

Nielsen's home turned out to have six remote controls with 239 buttons to choose from. (I checked our home and found seven cluttering our coffee tables.)

Nielsen looked at his four primary ones. These included the one for his DVD player, another for the TV, another for the replay TV recorder and another for his cable TV box, for a sum total of 160 buttons.

First came the dozens of inscrutable labels. Buttons named Angle, FAV and Condition challenged Dr. Nielsen to a degree he considered unreasonable.

Color contrast was another target. "It's truly annoying that so many remote controls have very low color contrast between the labels and the background, making them hard to read under poor lighting conditions," he said.

Furthermore, said Dr. Nielsen, too many of the buttons are identical in shape and color, differentiated only by their labels, which can be hard to read.

Then he took aim at the way numbers are laid out for channel selection. Dr. Nielson strongly favors a telephone keypad layout. "People already have a feel for a telephone keypad," he said.

Dr. Nielsen was struck by the lack of universal standards for remotes, most noticeable when it comes to the simple power button. "The Number One feature is just to turn the thing on, and that's indicated in three different ways" on three different remotes, he said (from the *New York Times,* February 19, 2004, "A 'FAV' Button? Interface Guru Is Not Amused," by Katie Hafner).

Dr. Nielsen, and the rest of us, may not have to wait too long for a solution. A major software company is now working on a system to control all entertainment components using one easy-to-use interface.

Your Lean Product Architecture Step-by-Step

1. Map functions against your customer *Ilities*. Challenge all functions as to their real worth. Are they really delivering the value the customer wants? Should any functions be added?

2. Create a diagram of functions. Do this on the system level. Do this on the sub-system level after your system level architecture has been agreed upon.

This schematic will show what the product must do, not how it will do it. A fishbone diagram works well for doing this.

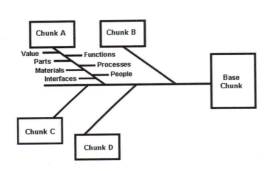

3. Group the functions into *chunks*, or sub-assemblies, or components. Clearly define the interfaces between the chunks. Think about how you will be sourcing each chunk.

Try to group like technologies. Consider maintenance and repair.

4. Create conceptual geometric sketches. This gives a pictorial view of the total system. Involve your suppliers. They will be able to contribute new ideas.

They will also be better able to understand the relationship between the chunk they are assigned and the total system.

Design components so that they can easily be reached for service. Avoid "shoebox" designs.

5. Do an *Ility and Ing Equation* check. Is the architecture lean enough? Is it really delivering the *Ilities*, or customer values? Is it really reducing *Ings*? Think about the *Three Sharks of Change*.

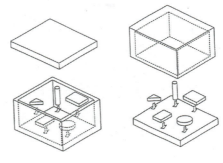

Is your architecture flexible enough to respond to changes in customer demand, technology improvements and competitor threats?

6. Refine interfaces and interactions. The boundaries between chunks are the interfaces. The interactions are the processes that flow across the interfaces. Do a detailed mapping of both interfaces and interactions.

Modularity will play an important role in designing your lean architecture. We will now turn to modularity in the section that follows.

(For an in-depth description of how to create your architecture, see David Cutherell's "Product Architecture" section in the PDMA Handbook of New Product Development, *221-233. See also Karl T. Ulrich and Steven D. Eppinger's* Product Design and Development, *(Irwin McGraw-Hill, New York, 2000.)*

Lean Design Solution Tool

Tool Name: *Product Architecture "Chunk Check"*

Purpose: Evaluate product design architecture's impact on the *Four Product Domains.*

Steps: 1. Stakeholders from each of the four product domains use the *Seven Evil Ings* to evaluate alternate designs for individual "chunks."

2. The goal is to surface a complete picture of a chunk's impact on all four domains.

3. These assessments are then used to begin understanding the trade-offs for product design improvement.

Evaluation of Chunk A

	Design Domain	Supply Domain	Manufacture Domain	Customer Use Domain
Complexity (Example)	Will require 50 percent new design/test effort	Existing supply chain can be used	No new processes	Enables easier servicing
Precision				
Variability				
Sensitivity				
Immaturity				
Dangerous				
High Skill				

Skill #5 – Modularize If It Makes Sense

Modularity is all the rage today. Outsourcing is the name of the game and modularity enables you to do this effectively.

But watch out. Modularity also has a downside. It makes it easier for your competitor to mimic your technology.

It can, in fact, turn components into commodities.

> You really want to know the secret to our success?
> It's simple. Legoability.
> — Dell Computer engineer

The general rule is to avoid embodying your product's differentiating elements in outsourced modules. This can be compared to giving away the farm.

What to modularize is dependent on the *Ility and Ing* strategy your team plans to deliver.

For example, Dell Computer's *Ility* strategy is to optimize *affordability, deliverability* and *maintainability*. While technical *performability* is assuredly on its list of primary customer values, it is not a key differentiator.

Dell's *Ing* strategy is to minimize the evil gremlins of *complexity* and *skill*. Dell's goal is to eliminate irksome steps in the *buying* and *servicing* your computer.

Dell's modularity strategy is aimed at outsourcing. Its designs are built on *functional* modules.

A prime example is the Dell computer I am using to write this book. Virtually every major component, from hard drive to snap-in battery, is modular. I benefit by being able to configure my laptop the way that suits me best.

Should I need service, I simply call in for the new "plug-and-play" component and FedEx delivers it the next day. I return my old component in the same carton.

Dell leaves the task of inventory maintenance to its modular component manufacturer, sparing themselves storage costs and obsolete shelf goods.

Most important, the task of technology innovation rests squarely with the supplier. This leaves Dell to focus on what it does best: creating the overall systems architecture and developing the market for their products.

By using modularity, Dell has created a far more flexible supply chain strategy, and has freed valuable resources so the company can concentrate on what it does best.

Another kind of modular strategy is to create *production* modules. These can be designed independent of their functions. Their primary purpose is to simplify factory floor operations.

Modularity Benefits

By clustering your parts into modules you give your product both design and manufacturing flexibility. It also can help you avoid massive product re-designs, in the future.

Clustering means an entire product need not be scrapped for simply one product feature change.

Modularity is a key strategy in applying the lean design *Law of Innovation Flow*. It can help you create a continuous stream of innovative product features.

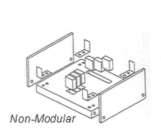

Non-Modular

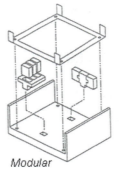

Modular

Modularity can bring major benefits to your company. Following are the *Eight Primary Company Ility Values* discussed in Chapter One and how a modular strategy helps deliver them:

Primary Values All Manufacturing Companies Seek	Potential Benefits
Profitability	Once design is complete, less design time and cost. Modules can be outsourced in competitive world market. Fewer internal *Ings*.
Investability	Module supplier carries cost of tooling and inventory. Supplier bears cost of new technology investment
Riskability	Risk of development transferred to supplier. "Legoability" makes it easier to overcome competitive threats
Produceability	Manufacturer can seek best supplier, focus his factory on what they do best. Easier assembly.
Marketability	Faster delivery. Lower cost. New features quickly switched in and out.
Growability	Manufacturer can focus on what will differentiate company in the marketplace. Product updates easier.
Leverageability	Resources freed up to enable manufacturer to focus on *Strategic Ility* differentiators.
Respectability	Use of modules from world class manufacturers enhances product line.

A modular outsourcing strategy, however, does carry with it some potential downsides such as:

- Product customization only possible with existing modules
- Product differentiation more difficult for manufacturer
- Module supplier may come to dominate production of component in world market, thus exerting control over the manufacturer

Modularity Customer Benefits

Modularity can bring major benefits to the customer. Following are the *Eight Primary Customer Values* and how a modular strategy helps deliver these values:

Primary Product Values All Customers Seek	Potential Benefits
Performability	Elimination of failures due to well-developed modules.
Affordability	Lower cost due to worldwide sourcing by manufacturer
Featureability	Functions and features can be added on a module-by-module basis
Deliverability	Faster product delivery. Easier specification and ordering.
Usability	Standard user interfaces. Modules made to worldwide standards.
Maintainability	Better replacement part service. Easier switch in and switch out
Durability	Confidence that modules are fully tested and proven in wider ranges of use. Quality high.
Imageability	User sees himself as making wisest choice re all of the above *Ilities*.

For the customer, however, product modularity does carry with it some potential downsides such as:

- Performance characteristics a customer seeks may not be available.
- Modular strategy requires each module to have an integrated physical structure, thus increasing weight and size.
- Modules subject to wear or require periodic replacement (example: printer ink cartridges) can be relatively high in cost.

Modularity Not Just for High Volumes

You don't have to be a high volume producer to benefit from modularity. Even low volume, slow-to-change industries are going modular.

Newport News Shipbuilding, America's biggest shipyard and builder of the U.S. Navy aircraft carriers and nuclear submarines is modularizing production.

Many components on the Navy's new attack submarine, being designed and built jointly by Newport News and General Dynamic's Electric Boat Division, are also done using modular design and build.

If modular outsourcing is so great for computer manufacturers, why aren't more companies getting on the bandwagon? The fact is that computers have a very fast *takt* time.

As I discussed with the *Law of Marketplace Pull*, the capacity to absorb change is far slower in some industries (war ships) compared to others (computers.)

Learning cycles in the computer industry are measured in months. Even in the auto industry, despite great strides in reducing design time, they are still measured in years. In the aircraft carrier business, it can take more than a decade to design a new fleet.

Designing products for modular outsourcing takes time and experience.

It takes confidence born of experience to convince a manufacturer to make the leap to modularity.

Modular outsourcing, while great in theory, is sometimes tough in the real world. It demands a new way of thinking, designing and working together with your supplier network.

Modularity Checklist

Modularity Must #1 – Require multi-generation conceptual designs.

As we learned with the *Law of Marketplace Pull*, all products begin to competitively erode the day they are launched. Some erode even *before* they are introduced to the market.

They are attacked by the *Three Sharks of Change* — customer preference, new technology and competitive threats. Look for suppliers who understand these forces and are anticipating them with continual design improvements.

Ask your supplier to show you how their design teams track each of these "three sharks" and how they are developing future product generations to deal with them.

Example: Toyota suppliers constantly provide prototypes that go far beyond current design requirements. They demonstrate that they are anticipating future customer needs. They are also showing they have the technology to meet those needs.

Modularity Must #2 – First simplify your product architecture.

Modular outsourcing begins with product complexity reduction. Make sure your functional strategy is well thought out first.

The basic rule is:

Simplify functions first, create modules second.

Modularity requires an "open systems architecture," the ability to integrate or "dock" components easily.

What is needed is a simple, clear product functional structure, including how each module will work and how its functions will be integrated with all others.

Your suppliers must be able to not only see how their component interfaces with your product, but also how it interfaces with the rest of your product's system.

Case in point: Over a decade ago we began working with automobile manufacturers on modular doors and even complete, modular interiors. It took years for such sub-systems to be finally outsourced.

The toughest challenge was the difficulty of assembling these modules to the vehicle itself. Vehicle door frames were notorious for being out of alignment, with few or no fixed positioning points.

Only when the problem of having a stable door-to-car-frame interface was solved was it possible to implement a modular door strategy.

Modularity Must #3 – Reduce the number of product variants.

Minimize the number of parts, sub-systems, or modules. Do this by encouraging your supplier to design more multi-functional modules.

Fewer modules mean fewer interfaces. Fewer interfaces means less opportunity for total system failure.

Fewer modules also mean a shorter, less complex supply chain. The end result can be simplicity up and down the product creation chain.

Modularity Must #4 – Start building long-term supply chain alliances early.

Modular outsourcing requires far closer supplier cooperation than traditional supply chain relationships.

Your partner must clearly understand your long-term product strategy, as well as your product system architecture.

Since design will drive the major part of outsourcing success, his design teams must be communicating with yours right from the start.

Think *end-to-end.*

You will be working on the total "end-to-end" process from concept to final customer. Your supplier's design teams must also be able to interface with other modular sub-system suppliers.

All of this means a high level of trust and complete understanding about mutual goals, something which does not happen overnight.

Remember: You will be designing not only a new product. You will also be designing a new logistics system. A key benefit of modular outsourcing is the chance to simplify the complexity of your supply chain.

Modularity Must #5 – Get your suppliers involved at concept stage.

The product concept stage is where the greatest gains can be made. Most of a product's success is determined at the early design stage. Trying to make a product modular in the late stages of product development is a tough task.

We encourage supplier and manufacturer teams to integrate their efforts right from the project's "Day One."

Invite trusted suppliers to participate in your first *Lean Design Kaizan.* This gets them participating in, and understanding, the entire product strategy before going to work on their individual modules.

Fundamental Rule: First design your process for how you and your suppliers' teams will work together. You should do this before you stand to design the new product. A good team process is the secret to eliminating problems later.

Modularity can help you reduce the number of parts in your inventory. But it may mean increasing the number of parts in your supplier's inventory.

Part count reduction is a tricky skill. In the next section, you will learn the "how to" of doing it well.

Skill #6 – Minimize Parts and Processes

Part count reduction is the most obvious of all lean design techniques. Not so obvious is process count reduction.

A non-existent part costs nothing to design, prototype, manufacture or service.

The same thing can be said for non-existent processes. A process you eliminate by design requires no time, costs nothing and will never result in a quality flaw.

> Our life is frittered away by detail. Simplify, simplify!
> — Thoreau

But be careful. There is skill in doing both part and process reduction well.

Reducing parts and processes can result in more complexity in the design that remains.

The *Complexity Gremlin* can have you spending more time and money on design, tooling, and manufacture, if the part is too complex.

Fewer parts do not always mean a better design.

Less parts can add counterproductive complexity to your project. You're trying to achieve an ever-elusive equilibrium.

It's a careful balancing act that takes skill. The purpose of this section is to help you develop that skill.

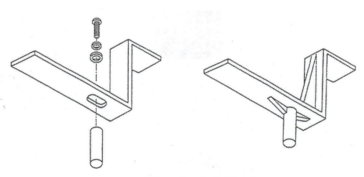

"Implode" Parts

How to Reduce Parts

You combine several parts into one part by "imploding" their functions. That is, you drive the functions of several parts into one part, thus eliminating them.

By combining parts, you typically will be able to minimize the number of things that can go wrong in your design. That is, if your new multi-functional part works as it should.

Part count reduction always brings with it a measure of risk. New parts can use new materials. New parts have different geometries. New parts need new design and testing.

Your car battery is a classic "win-win" case of a part count reduction effort that went right. Today's batteries feature "snap fit" caps, or in some cases, no caps.

Old designs had six screw type battery caps.

Customer benefits include:

- Fewer parts to handle
- Easier "snap fit" with less time required

Evolution of the Car Battery: A Part Reduction Success Story

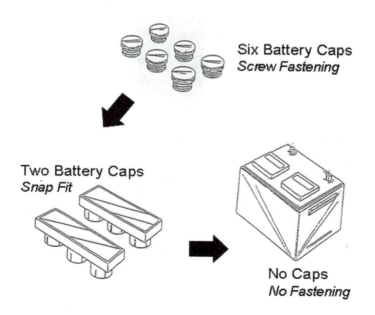

Six Battery Caps
Screw Fastening

Two Battery Caps
Snap Fit

No Caps
No Fastening

- Square or rectangular parts don't roll
- Larger space for "warning" label

Manufacturing domain benefits include:

- Fewer parts to manufacture, handle and ship
- Less tooling
- Less plastic material
- Bolder advertising label
- Easier packaging

Like all lean design solutions, there is no absolute black and white when it comes to part reductions.

If part integration is too complex, drawbacks can include:

- More design time and expense
- Higher tooling costs
- Less standardization
- Poor serviceability
- Higher risk

Like all lean design decisions, part count reduction decisions have to be held up *against your Ility and Ing Strategy that you developed with your Lean Design Mapping* effort, as described in Chapter Three.

Will the remaining part help or hinder the *Strategic Ilities*, or values, you are trying to deliver to your customer?

Will the complexity of the integrated part give the *Evil Ings* an opportunity to create waste?

Reducing Parts Step-by-Step

Here is an easy, step-by-step method for imploding parts:

1. List or sketch all of the parts in your design or subassembly.
2. Identify *all* of the functions that each part is performing. All parts perform two or more functions. No part ever performs a single function.

3. Simplify each functional statement by using a simple *verb/noun* description. For example: a threaded fastener securing Part A becomes "fastens Part A."

4. Link single or low function statements with verb/noun functional statements of other parts. Then visualize how this could be done geometrically.

5. When you run out of ideas, try "exploding" functions. This is unbundling functions from one part and transferring them to another part.

6. Evaluate your part count reduction ideas against your *Ility and Ing Strategy*. Will they reduce the seven *Evil Ings* that create most product waste? Will they enhance customer values, the Ilities that you need to delight your customers and differentiate your product?

Top Tips for Part Reduction

Here are some important tips on part count reduction:

Focus on "low functionality" parts first.

These are components that are not providing a lot of multi-functional value. Most fasteners fall into this category.

Low function parts are prime candidates for "implosion." The C-clip above is not multi-functional. It's difficult to install and is an opportunity for quality loss.

The snap solution eliminates the C-clip. However, it could drive tooling costs higher.

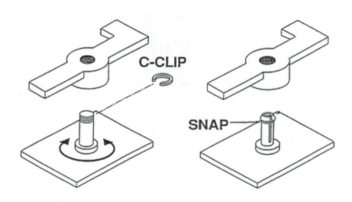

Try to eliminate moving parts.

Moving parts typically require more precision. They also require service as they can be subject to wear.

Re-use previous designs.

Try to use the same designs across many products. This reduces design time and risk.

Reduce part numbers.

Every part number requires documentation, control and, in most cases, inventory. Reduce the number of part numbers and you will eliminate both direct and indirect costs.

Specify off-the-shelf standard parts.

Standard purchased parts allow you to share tooling with your supplier's other customers. This also drives down your cost by driving up volume to your supplier. Off-the-shelf parts are highly cost effective.

Use Multi-Functional Materials to Reduce Part Count

New materials technology is now a big player in part count reduction. The most obvious example is the use of engineered plastics.

However, even using multi-functional materials must be done with a good deal of care.

Multi-functional materials are a favorite hangout of the waste-creating *Evil Ing Gang* you learned about earlier.

This is especially true for the *Gremlins* of *Complexity, Immaturity* and *Skill.*

Take for example the use of stainless steel. Stainless steel eliminates the need for paint (it's a part) and the variable process of painting.

A painted surface is a sensitive surface. It is easily damaged and requires a lot of packaging, protecting and, if you are not careful, a lot of repairing.

What about stainless steel for cars? It works for kitchen knives. Why not automobiles?

Maybe not. Adam Horowitz and the editors of the magazine *Business 2.0* recount in their book *The Dumbest Moments in Business History* the story of John DeLorean and his stainless steel gull-wing car.

Modestly named "The DeLorean," it was built in Ireland in the early eighties. This flashy sports car had two main selling points.

The first was the stainless steel body that did away with paint and rust. The second was the gull wing doors that opened by flipping upward.

The gull-wing doors proved to be a design disaster as drivers quickly learned they were very hard to close from inside the car.

But it was the stainless steel body that accelerated the downfall of DeLorean's brainchild. Stainless steel is expensive. However, stainless steel, as any good lean design engineer knows, is also heavy.

"Ostensibly a sports car, the lumbering DeLorean had a top speed of 75 miles per hour and went from 0 to 60 in about 10 seconds — closer to your uncle's Pontiac than a Porsche," Horowitz reports.

Typical Multi-Functional Materials

Here is a quick thumbnail guide to multi-functional materials and processes:

Material/Process	Characteristics
Composites	Integrates strength with flexibility in geometric shape
Engineered Plastics	Combines precision, finish, color and strength in one controllable process
Insert Molding	Combines dissimilar materials to produce a result greater than the sum of the individual parts
Co-Extrusion	Integrates different materials in same manufacturing operation
Cast Steels	Integrates strength and performance yet minimizes secondary machining operations
Powder Metal	Produces high precision in intricate shapes

Multi-functional Parts and Recycling

Using multi-functional materials and processes can sometimes come at a high environmental price.

This is especially true where recycling is concerned. Material integration may spell big problems downstream.

Multi-bonded products and insert molded components are not easily separated. They are extremely difficult to recycle.

Take for example the case of the juice box manufacturers who were caught in a big squeeze a while back.

Juice boxes – a mainstay of the lunch box – ended up in the limelight of an environmental controversy.

A ban on the boxes started in the state of Maine. Lawmakers there were convinced the juice box packaging — bonded paper, plastic and aluminum couldn't be easily recycled.

Packaging manufacturers fought back. The used boxes would be sent to a special recycling plant where they would emerge as plastic lumber.

Environmentalists were unimpressed. "They're trying to solve a problem backwards," said the Natural Resources Council of Maine.

"We'd like manufacturers to come up with a product that's easily recycled, rather than use these mixed materials," they said.

Process Complexity Reduction

If part count reduction stands out as the most obvious lean design technique, process count simplification ranks at the bottom as being the least obvious.

This is despite the fact that the processes needed to use a product can cost a customer many times that of his original purchase price.

Reducing complex lifecycle processes can pay even bigger design dividends than part count reduction.

Your customer's domain is fertile pickings for good process complexity reduction ideas. Every process step costs money, takes time and can result in a quality flaw.

Unfortunately, many of these process reduction opportunities are never harvested as they are not clearly visible to lean design team.

That is why the technique of using the *Seven Evil Ing Gremlins* to hear the *voice of your customer* is such a powerful communication tool. These seven characters start your customers talking about what they *don't like* about your product.

The *Evil Ings* give customers a framework of reference with which to express their dissatisfaction.

While a customer's internal processes are tough to see, most times seeing the internal processes in our own companies is just as difficult.

We have good ways to communicate knowledge about parts. Their geometric shapes appear on drawings.

Characteristics such as weight, strength and other data are easily expressed. The performance of parts is relatively easy to predict. Parts are visible.

Processes are hidden.

They are difficult to communicate. They are difficult to count. (Ever hear anybody give you an accurate "process count reduction"?)

They are difficult to predict. And they are difficult to get a handle on re cost.

Yet process complexity can account for 75 percent — or more — of a product's cost. The lean manufacturing revolution's greatest benefit has been in systematically attacking these "hidden factory" costs.

Consider this: even the most simple products can demand thousands of process steps. Compare this to the complexity of something such as a jet engine, and you can begin to understand why it takes years and millions of development tasks to bring a new jet engine to fruition.

Simply operating that jet engine requires thousands of processes or tasks to keep it in use.

Process Complexity Reduction Essential for Six Sigma

Design for Six Sigma is grounded in process complexity reduction. The enemies of Six Sigma are the *Seven Evil Ings*.

Each of the seven opens the door for potential quality loss. The *Gremlins* of *Variability, Immaturity* and *Skill* as especially harmful for any Six Sigma design effort.

The number of these kinds of processes in a design is a clear indicator of the difficulty, if not the impossibility, of achieving Six Sigma success.

The *Seven Evil Ings* were discussed earlier in this chapter. What I will share with you now are lean design techniques to attack these *Evil Ings* right at the start.

Manufacturing Domain Process Checklist:

- **Eliminate as many process steps as possible.** Every action takes time, costs money and, if not properly done, can result in a quality flaw.

- **Focus on the Seven Evil Ing processes.** These are the process families that will create the most problems on the factory floor. They offer a good framework for manufacturing folks to communicate specific processes that cause the most trouble.

- **Reduce the number of different technologies used.** Commonizing technologies will simplify everything from tooling to training.

- **Position highly variable processes early in your manufacturing sequence.** Design your product architecture so that parts that have a low quality potential do not carry other processes with them to the scrap bin.

- **Group like manufacturing processes in your product architecture.** Engineer your design so that it mimics the ideal on your factory floor.

- **Use easily processed materials and geometries.** Minimize the use of difficult to process materials. Use material geometries that are readily available. For example, round material typically costs less to purchase and process. Round parts cost less to tool and machine. Round parts are easier to assemble.

- **Reduce processing surfaces.** The ideal number of surfaces? None. Consider net shape components when it makes sense.

- **De-couple machine processes from human process steps.** This goes far in helping you meet OSHA requirements. It may also help you to more easily balance your production line.

- **Listen to your lean manufacturing champions.** Use what they tell you to design out or minimize the worst process problems they face.

Reduce Variable Processes

Customer Domain Process Checklist

- **Minimize the degree of skill required to both install and use your product.** Skilled personnel are expensive and sometimes hard to find. Reducing skill also reduces quality flaws.
- **Reduce or even eliminate the use of tools to install your product.** The ideal tool is the human hand.
- **Design wear parts to be easy to reach and replace.** Don't "bury" high service items to make them difficult to service.
- **Avoid adjustments.** Adjustments introduce variability into the use of your product.
- **Design for "open" servicing.** Try to design so that servicing is done from a single direction. Avoid "shoebox" designs. Minimize restrictive access.
- **Minimize precision needed for installation, use and maintenance.** Precision is difficult to maintain, especially when we human beings are called upon to deliver it.

Example of Precision Run Amok

Using precision parts can produce devastating results. This is especially true if inspection and test procedures are short-changed in the validation stage.

A major appliance manufacturer learned a hard lesson in its development of a new refrigerator compressor.

The project team designed two moving powder metal parts to work at a friction point of fifty-millionths of an inch – about one-hundredth the width of a human hair.

Nothing had ever been mass-produced as such an extreme tolerance.

The parts did not hold up in use. The cost: Over $450 million in replacement and service cost to correct the failure.

The Five Rules of Precision

1. Reduce precision as much as possible – open tolerances.
2. If you specify a precision tolerance, be prepared to pay for it.
3. Rely on machines for precision, not humans.

4. Control, inspection and test must be the constant companions of precision.

5. Reduce the number of precision surfaces to an absolute minimum.

Skill #7 – Simplify Assembly

One Christmas Eve long ago Santa Claus decided to give our young son a pedal car for being such a good boy.

I had the job of assembling this shiny red car. I began in the early evening, just after both our children went to bed with visions of sugar canes dancing in their heads.

I didn't finish until five hours and hundreds of parts later.

The *Gremlins* of *Complexity, Precision, Variability,* and *Skill* were constantly bedeviling me.

I will never forget that frustrating Christmas Eve.

Our son-in-law faced the same task for our grandson this past Christmas Eve. He got his son's car assembled in 30 minutes.

The difference? Lean design techniques such as design for assembly, a clear product architecture and the smart use of multi-functional plastic components.

Whether assembly is the last act on your factory floor or the first task in your customer's domain, it is where the quality battle can be won or lost.

Following are the *Five Primary Design for Assembly Techniques* you should know.

Don't Fight Gravity

Design for Z-axis top-down assembly. Don't fight gravity. Use it to your advantage.

Z-axis assembly helps part mating. By designing for top-down assembly you can also simplify your part handling and assembly tooling.

If Z-axis assembly is impossible, try to minimize the number of surfaces requir-

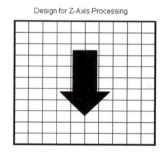

Design for Z-Axis Processing

ing assembly. Design so that assembly is done in sequential manner.

Try to avoid having to constantly reposition the product for assembly.

Imagine designing parts that ideally act like a neatly stacked deck of cards, all falling into place with a minimum need for labor or assembly equipment.

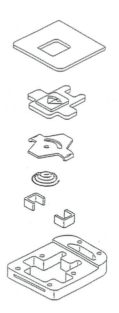

Assemble to a Rigid Base

Try to design your first part as a "fixture" to locate all other parts. Give it rigidity.

Design in "identification" features for positioning and retaining the parts that follow.

Try to use "self-locking" features that prevent parts from moving until they are finally secured.

Use Compliant "Funnel Features"

Part misalignment and tolerance stack-up can occur where different processes such as stamping, injection molding, casting and machining, many times all from different vendors, are to be mated.

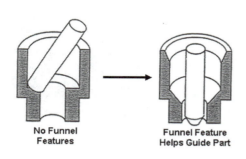

No Funnel
Features

Funnel Feature
Helps Guide Part

Compensate for misalignment by designing in "funnel features" that help guide parts into final position.

Such compliance techniques can be especially important for automated assembly.

Consider "Jig Saw Puzzle" Features

Always try to design for positive part identify.

Avoid assembly mistakes by designing parts with geometric features that mean they can be assembled in only one way — the right way.

Add external features to identify the correction orientation of a part. Such features can assure repeatability and avoid mistakes in human judgment

Color coding is a good technique. But care should be taken when using it for especially critical components.

Example: A major airframe manufacturer designed on-board fire-fighting equipment wiring to be assembled using color coding.

One near disaster revealed the aircraft's fire fighting system could fail in use.

Investigations later showed more than 50 percent of the systems were incorrectly assembled. The designers failed to use "puzzle assembly" techniques which would have made it impossible to assemble these key components incorrectly.

They were unaware that up to 20 percent of all humans are either partially or totally color-blind.

Minimize Fasteners

Try to reduce the number of fasteners in your design.

Fasteners are not multi-functional, require precision, and take skill to install – all archenemies of the lean design and production.

While their direct cost may appear low, they will drive "hidden costs" up to 30 times their purchased price.

Try to minimize the use of threaded fasteners. They carry a high potential for creating quality problems.

A lot of things have to go right for a threaded fastener to work well. Use high quality threaded fasteners.

The cost of cheap fasteners may be low but the hidden costs they can create are endless.

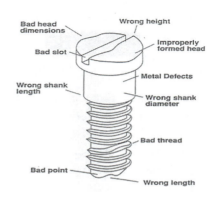

The Simple Screw?
Opportunities for poor quality.

Threaded fasteners demand a lot of processes. The *Complexity Gremlin* especially likes threaded fasteners.

The *Ings* they create include locating, drilling and tapping the hole for the fastener to go in.

Then there is aligning, inserting, driving and setting the fastener to the proper torque.

The Positive Side of Threaded Fasteners

Threaded fasteners sometimes take too much of a "bum rap."

Here are some benefits when you use them:

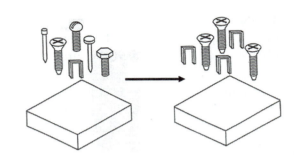

- **Service**.
  Threaded fasteners "communicate" well. They show you where and how to disassemble.
- **Risk**. Replacing them with "snap fits" or some other means of assembly can mean more risk in development and service.
- **Time to Market.** Integrating fasteners into parts takes design, development and test time. All of these are scarce when you are rushing to complete a product.
- **Repairability**. Breaking an integrated fastener can scrap a major component.

Reduce Fastener Complexity

If you can, use fewer fastener types to reduce complexity.

Using the wrong fastener is one of the most common assembly problems.

Minimize complexity further by reducing fastener counts

Eliminate differences in diameters, differences in head type, differences in lengths, and differences in material types. Try to "commonize" fasteners.

Doing this can increase fastener cost but significantly reduce warranty claims later.

Example: A boat manufacturer was experiencing high warranty claims for malfunctioning control panel lights. In several cases, customers were even electrically shocked.

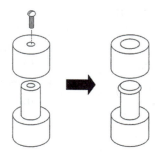

Screw Fastener Conversion to Snap Fit

The problem was eventually traced to one employee who used the wrong length fastener for securing components to the boat's panel. The fastener was cutting through the wiring bundle behind.

Had all the fasteners been specified to one length, the problem would have been avoided.

Snap fits can give you fits

Be cautious when replacing threaded fasteners with "snap fits."

"Snap-together" designs may eliminate fasteners and drive down assembly time.

But they can wreak havoc with your customer's patience when snap fits break or just don't fit well.

Snap fit designs also require more complex tooling, can take longer to design, and may involve you in more design risk.

How to Defeat the *Evil Ing* Gremlins in the Battle for Better Assembly

Evil Ing Gremlin	Design for Assembly Techniques
Complexity	Reduce number of parts and process steps required for assembly. Use common fastener types and sizes.
Precision	Use funnel or compliance features for part positioning. Avoid precision interfaces between parts.
Variability	Eliminate adjustments. Try to complete all assembly from one direction.
Sensitivity	Build to a rigid base part. Use "puzzle features" for orienting, positioning and securing components.

Immaturity

Avoid non-standard fasteners or unproven fastening techniques when customer assembly required.

Danger

Design out pinch points. Design for fewer assembly tools. Reduce human injury with less human assembly.

High Skill

Integrate skill into the assembly tool. Don't rely on consistent skill from the assembler. Use part identity features for "foolproofing."

Chapter 5

Lean Product Team Design *Kaizan*

In the first four chapters of this book you learned the "basics" of *The Lean Design Solution.*

- In Chapter One, you were introduced to the universal *Lean Design Equation.* It guides you in discovering the values your customers want, as well as helps you in eliminating product waste.
- In Chapter Two, you learned the *Five Laws of Lean Design.* Knowing these laws is essential for lean design success.
- In Chapter Three, you were introduced to *Lean Design Mapping (LDM).* This is a step-by-step method for bringing focus and direction to your lean design challenge.
- In Chapter Four, you learned the *Seven Lean Design Skills.* These are the skills you and your lean design team must know in order to solve the *Lean Design Equation.*

Now in this fifth and final chapter, you will learn how to conduct a *Lean Design Kaizan,* a way for harnessing all the above for maximum horsepower.

"*Kaizan*" is a lean manufacturing word. It's used to describe an intensive team effort to solve a manufacturing problem.

> New ideas seldom show up in old directions.

The same word is applied to the one day event for applying *Lean Design Mapping. LDM* is used as the format for the *kaizan.*

Your design team uses *LDM* to:

- Agree on the dimensions of your product challenge
- Create your "first draft" design strategy
- Surface new product design ideas
- Get management participation and buy-in
- Activate your product design feed-back system

In Chapter Three you were introduced to the "what and why" of *Lean Design Mapping.*

Now I will share with you the "how."

Who Should Attend

There is a well proven *Lean Design Solution* axiom that states:

If a stakeholder is not part of the design solution, they may become part of the problem later.

When conducting your *Lean Design Kaizan,* always err on the side of more, not less.

The first task in any design effort is to make sure you understand the design problem before you begin to solve it. We humans never see the same problem exactly the same way.

The full dimensions of your design challenge become clearer when you have a representative cross section of all those stakeholders who will eventually have to implement your design.

The format you will learn in the following has been used with as many as 100 participants. However, the ideal number is no more than 35 participants. This increases the quality of communication among participants.

There is no minimum number of participants. A *Lean Design Kaizan* has been held with as few as four participants.

Participants are broken down into smaller task teams, with no more than six persons on each team. These teams should be evenly balanced, as much as possible, by experience, skill and function.

There are six major tasks in a *Lean Design Kaizan.* Each team works the same task. They then report out their findings to the entire group.

Ideally, the *kaizan* should be completed in one day. Completion time is not driven by the complexity of the design task. It is driven by the number of participants.

Groups over 35 participants can require additional time with the *kaizan* extending into another day.

Kaizan Leadership

It's best to have a senior manager kick off the *kaizan.* This sets the tone and shows the importance attached to the team's effort.

The senior manager should explain:

1. Why the design project is important
2. What the benefits will be for the company
3. How the team members will benefit from their experience.

The team leader then follows and gives his understanding of the specific design challenge. This should also be done in writing prior to the *kaizan.*

However, never expect everyone in the room to have the same understanding of your challenge no matter how many times you communicate it.

I have never witnessed everyone agreeing on the same problem in all the years I have worked with product teams.

Ideally, a facilitator such as a Black Belt or lean design champion should be responsible for keeping the *Lean Strategy Mapping* process focused and on track.

This frees up the leader to focus on working with his team and better understanding their concerns.

An important part of the *kaizan* is to gain management participation and buy-in. The team leader should make arrangements for the entire team to report out their results to management immediately following the *kaizan.*

To have good collaboration, all participants must be trained in the basics of *The Lean Design Solution.* This can be done in a one-day session preceding the *kaizan* by the Black Belt or a lean design champion.

Computer based training is also available from the Institute for Lean Design.

Lean Design *Kaizan* Rules

A *Lean Design Kaizan* is governed by a set of *Lean Design Solution* rules. The leader, or facilitator, proposes each of these rules, in turn, to the participants.

He explains the benefit of the rule and then asks for the team's buy-in to it.

These are not to be pushed down a team's throat. They should be offered as a "code of conduct." Encourage your team to start creating their own additional rules.

Don't apply any rule unless there is 100 percent agreement.

I rarely find anyone challenging the use of these rules. All are grounded in common sense.

Rules set boundaries and focus energy. Lean design project teams welcome rules, especially when they have a role in setting them. Using the following rules will enable your team to move ahead rapidly with less wasted time.

(A complete set of these rules is in the appendix, "The 25 Most Valuable Lean Design Solution Rules.")

Following are some *Lean Design Solution Rules* to use:

Rule of Urgency

Never finish a lean design task on time.
Always strive to finish ahead of time.

Urgency breeds action. Set time limits for all tasks. Note that each of the tasks that follow has a time set for finishing it.

Time constraints create intensity and squeeze out waste. Deadlines help get jobs done. Time is your most precious resource. Use it wisely.

Tip: Always have a large clock in full view. Don't use your watch and be the "time cop." A clock on the wall is an impartial keeper of time.

Rule of the Titanic

Go problem seeking before problem solving. Never leave the dock before knowing where the icebergs are. Unknown obstacles sink the best of ships.

> Never leave the dock without knowing where the icebergs are!

You will never solve a problem you don't know exists.

Tip*:* Ask your team to write down their expectations and concerns *before* the *Lean Design Kaizan.* Don't try to answer all of these immediately.

Post them in full view and promise that each one will be addressed as quickly as possible during the course of your project.

Rule of Individual Thinking

Good individual thought is sometimes lost in the chaos of group discussion.

> Individual thought first, group discussion second.

Asking for individual thinking encourages total participation, the first step toward total buy-in.

Tip*:* Commit individual thought to paper. Ask team members to quietly write down their own thoughts on Post-It Notes and then share them with the entire team.

These can then be sorted on a flip chart and grouped into "families" of like ideas.

Writing ideas down also makes abstract ideas "real" and creates ownership.

Rule of Stakeholder Buy-In

Try to involve all those who eventually must help implement your project strategy They will understand the total challenge. They will also "own" the project.

> You never call your own baby ugly.

This can result in better support for your team's effort.

Tip: Poor stakeholder support is given as one of the major reasons for project teams failing. Cultivate it early by involving stakeholders at your strategy thinking stage.

Rule of Divide and Discover

> No two people ever see the same problem the same way.

Divide your team into smaller sub-teams, preferably with no more than six people on one team. Do this even with a small team.

Do this even when you have as few as four total participants. Create two teams of two people each. Ask each sub-team to work on the same problem simultaneously.

Why? Smaller teams increase the level of communication. Smaller teams improve the opportunity for deeper thought and discussion.

When the teams report out, the number of new and different ideas will amaze you. Sharing ideas among multiple teams surfaces new ideas and reveals common themes or problems.

Rule of Common Ground

> Agree on what you can agree on and then move on.

Start building your product strategy on a solid foundation of agreement. When completing any of the six *Lean Strategy Mapping steps*, agree on what the team can agree on.

Put tough issues into a "parking lot" to be revisited later.

Why? Don't get "wrapped around the axle." It is surprising how many tough issues begin to melt away when the focus is on agreement, not disagreement.

Rule of Consensus

Don't seek consensus too soon. Use the *Rule of Common Ground* to build agreement on the design problem first.

Tip*:* Don't expect to reach consensus on all issues. The purpose of your *Lean Design Kaizan* is not to immediately solve all problems.

> Consensus on the problem must precede consensus on the solution.

The purpose is to solve some, surface others and get the process of creating a successful product quickly moving forward.

The Rule of Iteration

Generate a lot of ideas. There is nothing as dangerous as only a few ideas.

The *Lean Design Mapping* process focuses innovative thinking. It creates boundaries and gives direction to the idea generation process.

> Your first design solution is never the best one. Your last idea is only a step in a continuous journey.

However, no design is ever "perfect." The relentless attack of the *Three Sharks* on your design assures this.

Rule of Product Design Feedback

Make sure you are getting feedback, which is important for your product's success. This means you must be measuring each of your design iterations against your product's *Strategic Ilities* and *Evil Ings*.

> That which gets measured gets attention.

Lean Strategy Mapping shows you how to create your product feedback system so that you can make meaningful comparisons and decisions.

Rule of Inertia

> A body at rest tends to stay at rest.

Get your design team into motion fast. Your team must demonstrate accomplishment at the end of their *Lean Design Kaizan.*

Lean Strategy Mapping helps you create a 90-day action plan focused on solving your *Ility and Ing Equation.* Everyone gets headed in the right direction.

Go for some *quick wins.* They build team morale, strengthen management buy-in and improve stakeholder confidence.

The Last Rule of Rules

> Those who help write the rules will be inclined to use them.

Rules imposed from on high are seldom faithfully followed. Encourage your team to write their own rules.

A team that writes their own rules will better understand them and abide by them.

Lean Design *Kaizan* Agenda

There are six steps in a *Lean Strategy Mapping Kaizan* event. Each of these steps follows a logical pattern of thought.

Each step first requires individual thinking, then group discussion and finally some form of agreement. This pattern is followed through out the *kaizan.*

All steps are bounded by time. The time given for each step should never be less than 30 minutes and never more than 45 minutes.

Reason: It takes a team a minimum of 30 minutes to individually think about the task requirements, discuss them as a group and then reach a conclusion.

Taking more than 45 minutes for a task usually is counterproductive. After that amount of time, teams begin to lose intensity and focus.

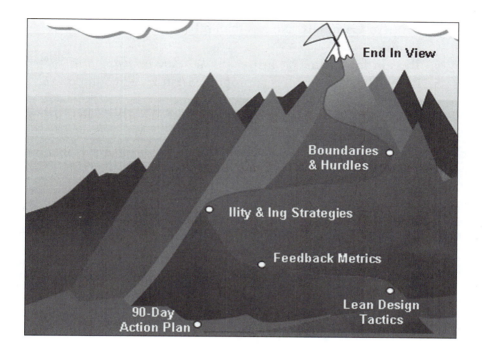

The team report out time is always in addition to the above limits. Each team should be given a maximum of five minutes, *preferably less,* to deliver their report.

Report outs should always be delivered with flip charts, overhead foils or computer projectors. Visuals reinforce communication. They also make data collection easier.

A support person or team member should be responsible for collecting all the data presented after each of the six tasks. This should *not* be the job of the facilitator or leader.

Before each of the six tasks, the leader or the facilitator should clearly explain five things. These should also be written on a flip chart or projected from a computer for added emphasis and clarity.

Never assume all participants will understand all of these same things in the same way. I have never seen this happen. Encourage questions about each of the five elements of the task.

1. **Task Description.** Simple verb-noun bullet statement(s)
2. **Deliverables.** Results posted on a flip chart or projected from computer

3. **Time to Complete.** No less than 30 minutes, no more than 45 minutes
4. **Reason for Task.** The answer to *"Why are we doing this?"*
5. **Rules That Apply.** Most appropriate Lean Design Solution rule.

Each of these five elements are given for the six Lean Design Mapping steps described below.

Here are the six *Lean Design Mapping* steps. A detailed explanation follows this thumbnail sketch.

Lean Design *Kaizan* Tasks	Purpose
1. End-In-View	Aligns team with project objectives
2. Boundaries and Hurdles	Defines innovation space and major obstacles
3. Ility and Ing Strategies	Focuses customer values, identifies worst waste
4. Feedback Metrics	Creates feedback system for evaluating designs
5. Tactics	Builds structure for innovation process
6. 90-Day Action Plan	Gets team delivering results quickly

The examples shown are taken from a case study entitled "Airline Seating Solves the Lean Design Equation."

The case describes an imaginary product team's effort to design a new line of high quality, low cost commercial airline seats called "Stratus."

While the Airline Seating Company (ASC) is an imaginary composite of several commercial seating companies, the problems they faced and the solutions they found are very real.

Lean Strategy Mapping Task #1: End-In-View

It's tough to attain what we cannot see ourselves doing.

That's why *Lean Design Mapping* begins with an imagined future state and then works back to the present for a solution.

It's like climbing a mountain backwards. Thinking about what future success looks like acts as a catalyst for action.

This first step challenges your team to begin to agree on your *end in view*.

You may find a wide range of misunderstanding, confusion and even disagreement about the *end in view*. This may be despite all your best efforts at clearly communicating what your project is all about.

Your goal is to clarify the design problem and get the mutual agreement of all team members, including management.

Don't expect to gain total agreement on the dimensions of your task with this first step. What you want to understand is the *diversity of disagreement*.

This is in line with the common sense notion that *"We will never work on solving a problem we don't know exists."*

And the corollary to that thought, *"We only imperfectly solve a problem we understand imperfectly."*

This first task has your team beginning to understand the "What, Why and When."

There will be a tendency for some participants to try to solve the design challenge (the "how") at this early stage. Try to immediately discourage this.

End-In-View Task Outline

Purpose	Begin to align design team with the project goals. Get all stakeholders agreeing on a common purpose.
Task Description	Sub-teams agree on "What, Why and When," of the project not "*How.*"
Deliverables	Bullet statements for "What, Why and How." Post on flip chart for review with other sub-teams.
Time to Complete	30 minutes for the team task. Time to report out will vary with number of sub-teams.
"Why Are We Doing This?"	Surfaces "disconnects" between team members, raises new questions not previously asked.
Rules to Use	Rule of Stakeholder Buy-In. *"You never call your own baby ugly."* Rule of Individual Thinking. *"Individual thought first, group discussion second."*

Traps to Avoid	Avoid *"duck diving"* down to technical requirements. Encourage defining general direction of the task, not a precise destination.

The Stratus example:

What:	Develop a new product platform of seating that reduces cost by a minimum of 25 percent and improves quality to Six Sigma levels.
Why:	Maintain Airline Seating's leadership position in the marketplace
When:	Ship new Stratus platform to first customer within 12 months, a 50 percent reduction in design-to-shipment time.

Task #2: Boundaries and Hurdles

No painting ever begins on an unlimited canvas.

You are as fast to design completion as your biggest bottleneck will allow.

This second task challenges your team to take a realistic view of the design challenge. It "frames" the limits of what can — and cannot — be done.

Your team is challenged to define hurdles early so that prompt action can be taken to solve them.

Boundaries and Hurdles

Purpose	Surface boundaries and hurdles, both technical and political. Boundaries define the "solution space" of the design effort. Hurdles identify problems the team must overcome.
Task Description	Bullet points on boundaries and types of hurdles. Identify all challenges, both technical hurdles and political hurdles.
Deliverables	Bullet statements on flip chart.
Time to Complete	35 minutes. Time to report will vary with number of teams.

"Why Are We Doing This?"	Begins to build team ownership of all boundaries and hurdles. Surfaces unknown hurdles. Challenges limits of the design boundaries or "solution space."
Rule to Remember	Rule of the Titanic. *"Never leave the dock without knowing where the icebergs are!"* Rule of Divide and Discover. *"No two people ever see the same problem the same way."*
Traps to Avoid	Tendency for product teams to impose constraints that really do not exist. Tighter constraints can limit creativity in finding design solutions.

ASC Stratus example:

Boundaries

- Must ship Stratus within 12 months
- Minimum 25 percent cost reduction
- Six Sigma quality level
- Minimum 50 percent less maintenance time

Hurdles

- Design resources stretched
- Supplier quality issues
- Limited certification time
- Customer styling buy-in uncertain

Task #3: *Strategic Ilities* and *Evil Ings*

Innovation requires strategic foresight.

Foresight is the ability to take an imaginative leap into the future and then come back to the present in the quest for good execution.

This is a three-part task:

(1) Using the *Eight Primary Customer Values* as a starting point (see Chapter Two, "The Law of Strategic Value"), each sub-team brainstorms and agrees on the six to eight most important product values needed for the success of your product. These *Ility* terms should be customized to fit your particular challenge.

While there may be as many as 25 to30 values you will incorporate into your design, typically these six to eight will be the primary drivers of your success.

Why only six to eight values?

It's far better to be exceptional at a few key *Ility* values than good at many things.

Strategy is all about simplicity. Complexity is difficult to understand and harder to implement. Complex strategies are usually doomed to failure right from the start.

Psychologists will also tell you that the average human mind cannot deal with more than about seven units at a time.

This is why seven is the popular number for lists that have to be remembered. We have seven digit phone numbers. There are Seven Wonders of the World. We play seven-card stud. And then there is Walt Disney's Snow White and the Seven Dwarfs.

Feel free to invent *Ility* words. Choose unique ones to more clearly describe the value your customer seeks. Keep them simple. Big, competitive ideas almost always come in small words.

Then get all your fellow team members to help define these unique value definitions. This is far better than using a generic term with each team member having a different definition in mind.

The use of unique terms also encourages your stakeholders to make sure they know what your team really is seeking to deliver.

An example is *legoability*, a term used by Microsoft to mean the ability to upgrade a product without having to reinvent the wheel. Modularity is an important part of that company's value strategy.

(2) Using the *Seven Evil Ings* as a framework of reference (see Chapter Two, "The Law of Waste Prevention"), ask each member of the team, including other stakeholders, to describe the worst examples for each of the *Seven Evil Ings* for the existing product (or for the competitor's product).

Go well beyond the factory floor in search of examples. Look at the design process, the supply chain, and the customer's domain as well as your own factory.

Remember: You will be unable to do this without having your marketing, sales, and field service stakeholders in this crucial meeting.

Brainstorm many values, but finally decide on six to eight *Ilities*. *Why stop at eight?* Because this is the limit of what a multi-functional team can trade-off at one time. Focusing on a maximum of eight *Ilities* enables your team to concentrate on the important few, not the trivial many.

(3) Following report outs by each sub-teams, have all sub-teams meet as a group and reach consensus on one set of strategic *Ilities*. Using the *Rule of Common Ground* and under the direction of the team leader or lean design champion, the entire group agrees on the first cut of *Strategic Ilities*.

Strategic Ilities and Evil Ings

Purpose	Identify the "critical few" *Ilities* your team must deliver to be successful. Identify the worst examples of the *Evil Ings* you need to avoid in your new design.
Task Description	(1) Each sub-team agrees on their six to eight *Ilities*. (2) Sub-teams agree on worst examples of *Evil Ings*. (3) Sub-teams then meet as a total group and use consensus to agree on one set of *Ilities*.
Deliverables	Bullet definitions for each *Ility*, prevention targets for worst *Ings*.
Time to Complete	35 minutes for *Ilities*. 35 minutes for *Ings*. Sub-teams report out following each of the two tasks. 15 minutes for reaching consensus on key *Ilities*. This is done following report outs.
"Why Are We Doing This?"	A clear strategy for delivering key values (*Ilities*) and preventing the creation of waste (*Evil Ings*).
Rule to Remember	Rule of Common Ground. *"Agree on what you can agree on and then move on."* Rule of Consensus. *"Consensus on the problem must precede consensus on the solution."*

Traps to Avoid

Failure to adequately define each of the key *Ilities*. Not having the right stakeholders on hand to understand the scope of the total design task. Getting hung up on reaching consensus on the "first cut" of the strategic *Ilities*.

ASC Stratus *Strategic Ilities*

Strategic Ility Values	Team Definition
Marketability	New line to be #1 preferred brand
Affordability	Best value/cost producer
Manufacturability	Meet or exceed factory cost goals
Deliverability	Deliver when customer want seats
Reliability	Best in class rating
Maintainability	Easiest to maintain of all competitors
Functionality	Exceed customer expectations

ASC Existing Product Line *Evil Ings*

Evil Ings	Examples
Complexity	In excess of 1500 unique seat part numbers
Precision	Precision adjustments on everything from seat recliners to tray tables
Variability	150 unique seat models
Sensitivity	Inability for many components to take rough abuse
Immaturity	Use of some new materials that didn't perform as expected
High Skill	35 unique custom seat programs going on at the same time.

Task #4: Create Feedback System

The purpose of this step is to develop a feedback system to track how well you are doing on delivering results. Measurement enables your team to clarify your objectives and convert these to a set of measurable outcomes. This follows the *Rule of Fast Feedback* discussed in Chapter Two.

Performance improvement requires three metrics. The first is a goal. The second is a starting point or "baseline." And the third is a process for tracking how well you are performing in reaching the goal.

Create Feedback System

Purpose	Create system for tracking performance in delivering *Strategic Ility* goals and preventing *Evil Ing* complexity and waste. Get input from all stakeholders on their perspectives about the team's "starting point" or the "as is" of the existing design.
Task Description	Using a scale of 1-10, sub-teams calibrate or "baseline" existing product's performance (or the competitor's product) again the new *Strategic Ilities* selected in the Step #3 above. Likewise, the existing product is also measured for its performance against the *Evil Ings*. Team members must explain the "why" of each rating. Calculators are banned in reaching a sub-team description. The key point of this first step is the exchange of views, not a precise number. *(See Chapter Four for the step-by-step way to do this.)*
Deliverables	Sub-teams report out "as is" baselines for both *Strategic Ilities* and *Evil Ings*. Group meets as a whole to discuss variances between sub-teams. Group agrees on a "first cut" baseline.
Time to Complete	45 minutes. This does not include report out time and discussion. Time to report out results will vary with number of teams working independently.
"Why Are We Doing This?"	(1) Begins to get everyone on the same page re the team's starting point. (2) Surfaces different points of view (3) Begins to get buy-in to

ongoing way to measure total product design performance and conduct trade-offs.

Rule to Remember   Rule of Product Design Feedback. *"That which gets measured gets attention."*

Traps to Avoid   Tendency for sub-teams to short cut the task and arrive at a number by calculating a sub-team average. The rating for each *Ility* and *Ing* is not as important as is the process for arriving at that number.

Rating	Ility Value Level
9-10	Extremely High Value. Sets the standard for the industry
7-8	High Value. Superior to that of most competitors
5-6	Acceptable. Meets expectations most of the time
3-4	Low Value. Frequently does not meet expectations
1-2	Extremely Low Value. Well below that of all competitors

Ratings shown are for current ASC seating line.
Scale: 10 = *Ility* level sets standard for the industry

Strategic *Ility* Values	Rating	Reasons Why
Marketability	4	Losing market share to aggressive overseas competitor offering new product line
Affordability	6	No longer low cost producer due to high cost of components
Manufacturability	7	Improving due to lean manufacturing but gains now at a standstill due to design complexity
Deliverability	7	Improving due to lean manufacturing but component non-standardization stalling further gains
Reliability	8	High but design complexity and precision required for maintenance continues to be a problem
Maintainability	6	Customer complaints about amount of skill and time required to service seats
Functionality	6	Competitor seat offer new features such as faster fabric change out.

Rating	*Ing* Waste Level
9-10	Intolerable. Highest level in industry
7-8	Excessive. Worse than most competitors
5-6	Tolerable. High but controllable
3-4	Low. Minimum impact on cost and quality
1-2	Extremely Low. Well below that of all competitors

Ratings shown are for current ASC seating line.
Scale: 10 = *Ility* level sets standard for the industry

Evil Ings	Rating	Reasons Why
Complexity	9	More than 1,500 unique seat part numbers creating chaotic serviceability. Most complex product line in airline seating industry
Precision	8	Precision adjustments on seat recliners and tray tables constant source of customer maintenance complaints. Precision now seen as creating unneeded waste
Variability	8	150 unique seat models taxing engineering and sales time. Also source of customer confusion
Sensitivity	6	Many fabric components unable to take tougher abuse due to longer replacement cycles. Complaints increasing
Immaturity	6	Use of some new materials that didn't perform as expected has eroded customer confidence
High Skill	7	35 unique custom seat programs going on at the same time has engineering staff stretched to the limit

Task #5: Design Tactics

With this task your team moves from problem understanding to problem solving. The goal is to get new design tactics out on the table quickly. This gives your design team an opportunity to flex their "creative muscle."

People resist that which is confusing and cherish that which is simple. Seek to simplify your product first.

Generate as many ideas as possible. The road to simplicity is hard work.

This step is only the beginning of your team's innovation process. The

> All life is an experiment. The more experiments, the better.
> — Ralph Waldo Emerson

goal here is to set in motion a disciplined process for doing this innovation so that a greater number of focused ideas can be generated.

See *The Law of Innovation Flow* in Chapter Two and the *Five Lean Targets of Opportunity* described there for a way to systematically brainstorm new ideas.

Design Tactics

Purpose	Start the creative process of seeking innovative design solutions. Give team members an immediate sense of accomplishment. Provide direction for future innovation efforts.
Task Description	Using the *Five Lean Targets of Opportunity* to kick start innovative thinking, team members brainstorm ideas for each. Brainstorm as many tactics for delivering each *Strategic Ility* and preventing each *Evil Ing* as possible.
Deliverables	Bullet statements and sketches of design ideas. Report outs by each sub-team should explain how each idea.
Time to Complete	45 minutes. Time to report results will vary with number of teams working independently.
"Why Are We Doing This?"	Surface team member innovative ideas. Start collaborative process of innovative idea sharing.
Rule to Remember	Rule of Iteration. *"Your first design solution is never the best. The last is only a step in a continuous journey"*
Traps to Avoid	Use of random versus focused brainstorming to generate new ideas. Tendency for team to want to close off innovation process early and "get on with the real work of implementation."

Some of Airline Seating's design tactics.

Five Lean Targets of Opportunity

Targets	Stratus Team Design Tactics
Functions	*Add* rear mounted foot bar, cup holder, PC power port and USB port. Design tray for quick detachment and zero adjustments
Parts	*Reduce* stock levels by designing one seat platform with interchangeable parts
Lifecycle Processes	*Eliminate* variability of Velcro fastening with "snap fit" fastening
Materials	*Substitute* aluminum back plate for fabric seat backing to overcome aft passenger intrusion problem
People	*Reduce* number and skill of maintenance people with modular design

Task #6: 90-Day Action Plan

Ideas have a short shelf life. You have to act on them before their expiration date.

This *Lean Design Kaizan* step gets your design team quickly into motion.

With this final step your team agrees on a 90-day action plan for moving your design effort forward.

Forward motion creates agility. Try steering your car while parked!

Your team must agree on which strategies make the most sense. Your team then sets up a plan to get these strategies in motion.

90-Day Action Plan

Purpose	Create a "first step" action plan approved by the team, management and stakeholders. Gets your team off the mark quickly and builds confidence.

Task Description	Sub-teams and then entire team agrees on the "What, Who and When" of most important 90-day tasks.
Deliverables	List of tasks with who is responsible and when due. Also list of "open issues" that have to be researched and resolved.
Time to Complete	35 minutes. Time to report results will vary with number of teams working independently.
"Why Are We Doing This?"	Overcomes inertia. Gives team confidence they are off the mark and moving. Enables team to validate direction of their strategy.
Rules to Remember	Rule of Urgency. *"Never finish a lean design task on time. Always strive to finish ahead of time."* Rule of Inertia. *"A body at rest tends to stay at rest."*
Traps to Avoid	Tendency to want to develop a detailed plan for entire product development effort.

Management Report Out

The entire team reports out their proposed product strategy to management, and as many stakeholders as possible, immediately following their one-day *LeanDSM Kaizan*, the next morning or as soon as possible.

> Ideas are useless unless used. The proof of their value is their implementation. Until then they are in limbo.
> — Theodore Levitt

The presentation format is a 30-minute review of all six steps of the *LeanDSM Kaizan*. This clearly shows management the logic of how your team arrived at your strategy. Management should be asked to withhold questions until the team presents all six *LeanDSM* points.

Avoid a "serial" report out, presenting to one manager at a time or having managers review the results of the *LeanDSM Kaizan* individually. A major purpose of the group presentation is to surface disconnects or disagreements between managers and/or stakeholders.

Following the presentation, the team should have a clear picture of management's degree of understanding and support. The *LeanDSM Kaizan* gives a "big picture" view for everyone to align their individual efforts to.

Strategy Presentation to Management

Purpose	Get management and stakeholder buy-in to your product strategy. Surface disagreements between managers. Demonstrate team unity.
Task Description	Team leader delivers results of Step #1, *End-in-View* and the final Step #6, *90-Day Action Plan.* Other team members deliver Steps #2 to #5.
Deliverables	Management and stakeholders given a high level 10 to 12 page handout describing results of all six steps. Management asked to buy into the strategy or give ideas for changing it. Team leader should "ask for the order" at the end of the 30 minute team presentation.
Time to Complete	Presentation should take 30 minutes maximum. Management and stakeholders words missing here? without questions until end of formal presentation. Maximum 30 minutes more for questions and challenges. Total meeting should last no more than 60-90 minutes.
"Why Are We Doing This?"	Builds management confidence in the product team's strategy. Builds team confidence that management understands their strategy and will support it.
Rule to Remember	The Last Rule of Rules: *"Those who help write the rules will be inclined to use them"*
Traps to Avoid	Tendency of managers to want to interrupt presentation to prematurely voice their views. Tendency of team members to give too much detail.

Summary of Lean Design *Kaizan*

Lean Design Mapping Steps	Tasks	Why?
Pre-Work	Train all stakeholders in Lean *Design Equation* and *The Five Laws of Lean Design*. Ask all stakeholders to think about what *Ilities* they want to see in the design and what *Ings* they want reduced.	Gets all stakeholders on a level playing field. Gives stakeholders an active role in both understanding Lean Design and participating in the strategy creation process.
Kaizan Purpose	Complete first iteration of the lean design mapping process and deliver "first cut" to management team.	Enables a Day One holistic or Big Picture view of the entire challenge and the roles stakeholders must play.
Task #1. End-In-View	Gain agreement on the "What, Why, and When" of the design challenge.	Orients team toward one destination and frames the timeliness of the task.
Task #2. Hurdles	Identify the "solution space" and surface all hurdles, both technical and political.	Surface boundary definition inaccuracies. Define hurdles clearly to overcome them early.
Task #3. *Ility and Ing* Strategies	Starting with the *Eight Primary Customer Values*, agree on the six to eight values that will delight customers and satisfy your company. Using the *Seven Evil Ings*, have all stakeholders give worst examples of each for the existing (or competitor's) product.	Creating a value strategy focuses team on values that will differentiate their product from the competition and solve urgent customer needs. Crafting a waste prevention *Evil Ing* strategy enables product to deliver value with minimum cost and maximum quality.
Task #4. Feedback Metrics	Baseline the "as is" of your current (or competitor's) product using the *Strategic Ilities* and *Evil Ings* you identified in Step #3.	Enables the design team to understand where they are starting from and the dimensions of the task they face.
Task #5. Design Tactics	Brainstorm as many tactics for delivering each *Ility* and preventing each *Ing* as possible during the task time.	Gets existing solutions "out on the table." Gives the design team an opportunity to flex their creative muscle.
Task #6. 90-Day Action Plan	Agree on a "What, Who, When" 90-day action plan. Review *Open Issues* not resolved or that await answers.	Overcome inertia. Gives team opportunity to validate their strategy.
Management Report Out	Entire team reports out to management in a 30 minute presentation at end of day or the next morning.	Shows unity of the team. Shows the logic of the team's thinking. Surfaces "disconnects" between managers.

Staying On Course

In the next chapter, I will give you a way to keep your team on the right course. You will learn how to create *Lean Design Scorecards*.

These are created each time a new design solution is being considered. The new design is rated against your team's *Ility and Inq Equation*.

Lean Design Scorecards give you a way to compare many different design solution sets. They are an efficient, quick way to capture team knowledge.

They also give every stakeholder a role to play in the design development process.

Chapter 6

Lean Design Scorecards

It's been said that bad measurement kills more new product efforts than any other single reason.

An example: A major pump manufacturer tracks the progress of its new product design using the "common three" metrics of cost, technical performance and schedule. The design team performs successfully on all three.

> Son, remember this. Never get into anything when you don't know how to keep score. You're bound to lose.
> — John Huthwaite, Sr.

But only when they are ready to go to market do they discover that "installability," the ease of installation, is the customers' primary need.

Their competitor recognizes the need and changes its design equation to focus on the strategic value of low installation time and skill.

They design the "EZ-2-Install" pump line and capture market share with a design that can be installed in half the time.

Measure What Is Important

There's an old saying that goes:

Measure the right things and get the right results.
Measure the wrong things and get the wrong results.

You will recall from Chapter One the *Law of Fast Feedback*. It says that we must measure the *Strategic Ility Values* customers really want.

It also encourages us to measure how well we are reducing the impact of the *Seven Evil Ings*. These are the design solutions that create most quality and cost problems.

When you apply *Lean Design Mapping*, the technique used in the *Lean Design Kaizan* described in the previous chapter, you will be surprised by the number of new design solutions.

One of your immediate tasks is to make sure you are using a good compass to see which of these solutions will take you in the right direction.

Please note I use the word "compass." You should first make sure you are heading in the right direction. Later you can "fine tune" your measurement system to make it more precise.

In Chapter Three we described how *Ility* and *Ing* spider charts can be used to quickly compare many design solutions. In this chapter you will learn the "How To" of using spider charts to create *Lean Design Scorecards*.

Lean Design Scorecards can be easily integrated into your existing product measurement system. Or they can be used as "stand alone" metrics.

Helps You Share Knowledge

In his excellent book *Product Development for the Lean Enterprise*, (The Oaklea Press, Richmond, Virginia, 2003) Michael Kennedy emphasizes how Toyota uses a "knowledge based" approach to product design. He sees this as a fundamental reason for Toyota's consistent success.

Kennedy sees encouraging, sharing and applying collective knowledge as everyone's task. It is, he says, the key to product development success.

Lean Design Scorecards are an easy, quick way to capture product knowledge. They measure the total "leanness" of your product design.

However, their greatest value is in the *process* of making the measurements. They provide a channel of communication between stakeholders in all the four product domains.

Lean Design Scorecards capture the knowledge behind the metrics. They enable you to see many possible design solutions in many different dimensions.

The process of knowledge capture is made up of three parts:

The new knowledge must be made explicit.

This is a process that has been called knowledge articulation.

This means it has to be captured in a way people can understand. It has to be presented in a *context* that is easily understood.

For example, the *Eight Primary Ility Values* provide a framework for categorizing what is good — or not so good — about a product solution.

Likewise, the *Seven Evil Ings* provide a context for communicating what is bad about a design solution.

Lean Design Scorecards with their *Ility* and *Ing* metrics give us a way to gather product knowledge in an organized manner. They are at a level where the information can be shared to make decisions about the entire product system.

Detailed information can be gathered under these classifications, without encumbering the total product decision making process.

The knowledge must be communicated.

Knowledge is useless unless there is a means for easily transferring it to other parts of an organization. While company intranets and guide books have been used for years to do this, many fail because the people for whom this knowledge is intended do not read this information.

There is a breakdown between the person communicating the information and the people who are supposed to receive it. As a workshop attendee once said, *"Somebody is pitching but no one is catching."*

Lean Design Scorecards overcome this communication breakdown. The scorecards are worthless unless all product stakeholders have shared in contributing their knowledge to create them.

Each proposed design solution must be rated by each stakeholder. However, the rating is only a means to the real end: *the explanation of why the rating is what it is.*

The scorecards give all stakeholders a *context* as well as a *framework* for communicating their knowledge. They enable the entire organization to "see" what is happening within the product development process.

The knowledge must be institutionalized.

There are two types of knowledge institutionalization. The first is through formal product data banks. The second is in the minds of employees.

The second is by far more powerful than the first. However the knowledge we humans have is subject to memory decay. We also take a lot of good knowledge with us when we leave or retire.

What Toyota does well is to prevent this memory loss and decay. It incorporates new knowledge into the broader organizational memory. Toyota uses simple, sometimes one-page data sheets to make valuable new information available to the rest of the organization. That knowledge is not lost when certain individuals leave or work teams disband or change.

I will always remember the liaison engineers from my Japanese partner Nitto Seiko working late into the night faxing back data sheets on product issues we were making at my machine tool company in Troy, Michigan.

Those Japanese engineers were institutionalizing what they were learning in their new United States machine tool market.

Scorecards have the same purpose. Data can be easily captured and stored for later retrieval.

They not only help make decisions but also *communicate the reasons* "*why.*"

Rule of "Ask Why Many Times"

"Why?" is a powerful word for getting to the "bottom of things." It forces us think about root causes.

It is the basis of the *Rule of the Onion* given to me by an aerospace engineer many years ago:

My Japanese friends are the ones who always remind me of the old saying *"Ask why five times."* The Rule of the Onion says go well beyond five if you must.

> Rule of the Onion: Keep peeling until you get at the truth no matter how much it makes you cry. Ask "Why?" many times.

The intent, of course, is to get to the root cause drivers that ultimately drive true knowledge.

Lean Design Scorecards are based on this kind of "onion peeling" thinking.

Predictive Measurement is Tough

Lean Design Scorecards use a technique called *predictive measurement.*

A metric is "predictive" when it forecasts a future state based upon data immediately at hand.

The opposite of predictive product metrics are *post-design* metrics. Post-design metrics in the *Manufacturing Domain* are such things as quality yields, actual processing time, and many others.

In the *Customer Domain,* they are mean time between failure, repair time, and others.

Measuring when the design is on the factory floor or in the field is relatively easy.

However, the horse has already left the barn. While we may have the "real" data at that point, making product changes to improve the numbers is difficult or even impossible.

Predictive measurement is the way the *Lean Design Solution* makes sure your design is on the right track before it even leaves the drawing board.

Many resist using predictive measurement because it lacks the precision and certainly of post-design measurement. It is too reminiscent of the "crystal ball" approach to decision making.

Predictive measurement is attacked as being too "subjective" or not "data driven."

Yet it is the most useful form of measurement as it enables us to take preventative action.

A Lesson from Your Doctor

The medical profession has successfully used predictive measurement for many years. Millions are living longer and more active lives because of it.

When you go in for a physical check-up you are quizzed on a number of "causal drivers."

These can range from "Do you smoke?" to "How much exercise do you have each week?" You are also weighed, blood tests taken, and a number of other check-ups done.

From this data your physician can tell you present state of "wellness." He can also look at actuarial data and tell you what might typically happen if you do not change some of your living habits.

He does this by using "predictive measurement." Your physician knows the causal linkages between the decisions you are making now and where they will take you in the future.

Lean Design Scorecards, the way the *Lean Design Solution* compares alternative design solutions, work in the same manner. They will tell you if your team is on the right track.

Lean Design Scorecards help assure your product will be a "healthy" one when it leaves the drawing board.

You can integrate them into your existing product measurement system. Or you can use them in a "stand alone" manner.

What Do Lean Design Scorecards Look Like?

Lean Design Scorecards must always be customized to meet your organization's unique needs. Formats will vary from company to company and even from team to team.

However, at their highest level all scorecards contain a minimum of *two basic types of information:*

Customer and Company *Strategic Value Ility* Ratings

This is a rating on how well a given design solution would perform compared to the six to eight *Strategic Value Ilities* your team has named as being most important.

The *Lean Design Mapping* technique described in the last chapter is the source of these *Ilities*.

All stakeholders individually first assign a *Customer Ility Value* rating for each solution.

They then give the reasons "why" for their rating. The purpose is to make stakeholder knowledge explicit or open to the view of the entire team.

For example, "affordability" can be seen in a very different way by someone from the *Manufacturing Domain* as opposed to one from the *Customer Domain.*

Manufacturing folks typically are focused on the cost of materials and the labor required to process and assemble them into a product. The goal is to make the purchase price as low as possible to keep competitive.

Customers care about the purchase price of a product but may be far more concerned about the fuel-like material required to use the product.

All stakeholders then assign a *Company Ility Value* rating for each solution. You learned about these *Eight Primary Company Ility Values* in Chapter One.

Once again, stakeholders must give the reasons "why" for their ratings. This again makes stakeholder knowledge open to the view of the entire team.

Potential Product Waste Rating

This is an evaluation on how well a given design solution performs on preventing each of the *Seven Evil Ings.*

As you will recall from the *Law of Waste Prevention* described in Chapter Two, these are the seven types of design solutions that create the worst quality and cost problems.

Each stakeholder rates the given design from the perspective of their domain.

For example, "complexity" in the *Manufacturing Domain* may mean an excessive number of parts.

However, "complexity" to those in the *Customer Domain* can mean tasks that are difficult to perform in order to use the product.

Another example is the *Evil Ing* of "precision." Precision on the factory floor can be the use of extremely tight tolerances when they are not really needed.

"Precision" for the customer, however, can mean the way the product requires tasks to be done in a precise sequence or manner.

Fast Feedback on Many Solutions

Using *Lean Design Scorecards* gives you a way to quickly look at many different design solutions.

They are especially useful for applying *Set-Based Design*, the Toyota practice described in Chapter Two. When applying set-based design you need a consistent, quick way to get feedback from all stakeholders.

Scorecards give you a way to look at many different iterations without wasting valuable team time.

Remember that the *Law of Innovation Flow* says that more iterations at a project's "front end" is always best. The need for costly changes and iterations at the back end will be far less.

Creating Scorecards

Lean Design Scorecards do not require added resources or time. They are created as part of the normal design development process.

There are three steps in using *Lean Design Scorecards:*

Step #1. Team Baselines *Ilities* and *Ings* of the "As Is" Product.

This may be your existing product. Or you may want to use your competitor's product.

This is first done from the individual viewpoints of stakeholders in the *Design, Supply, Manufacturing* and *Customer Domains.*

A *rating scale* of 1-10 is used with a "10" being world class excellence. (Many teams will ban the number "5" in order to prevent some from taking the "easy way out" with their assessment.)

Your team leader then captures all the rating and "whys" into a composite. All stakeholders then meet to share their ratings and reasons for them.

This meeting need not be done in person. The scorecard approach gives a well-structured framework for discussion. These knowledge sharing meetings can be done in a webcast or audiocast.

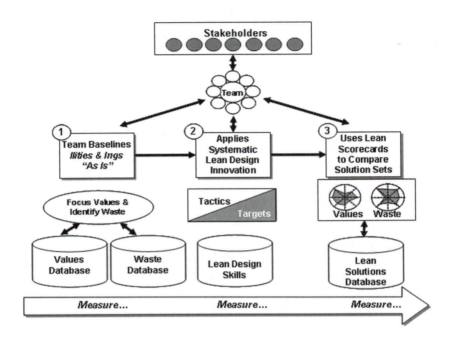

The primary purpose is to share knowledge, to make it *explicit.* These assessments are captured in a Values-Waste database for later retrieval and reference.

The team then agrees on a baseline rating for each of the *Strategic Ilities* and the primary reasons for these ratings.

Under the leadership of the team leader, the team agrees on a baseline rating for each of their six to eight *Strategic Customer Ilities.* The team takes the same approach in setting a baseline rating for their *Company Strategic Value Ilities.*

A baseline rating for the Seven Evil Ings is done in the same manner. A scale of 1-10 is used. However, in this case the number "10" means an extremely excessive amount of waste will be created by a given design solution.

These two measurements are displayed on spider charts. With the *Strategic Ilities* chart the goal is to fill the chart to try to reach a rating of "10." With the Evil Ing chart the goal is to shrink the size of the *Evil Ing* footprint.

Step #2. Team Applies Systematic Lean Design Innovation.

The team uses the techniques of *systematic innovation* (see Skill #3 in Chapter Four) to generate many different design ideas.

The *Five Product Targets* and the *Eight Primary Lean Design Tactics* are used to stimulate many different ideas.

All stakeholders are asked to contribute ideas. This moves a stakeholder from just *identifying* a product problem to having a role in *solving* that problem.

This step clearly communicates each stakeholder's responsibility for making the product a success.

Stakeholders are moved from being just *evaluators* to *contributors.* This is in line with the notion that if a stakeholder is not part of the solution, he may become part of the problem later.

It is also very difficult for someone to "call their own baby ugly."

These ideas are integrated into a portfolio of set-based design solutions by the core team. This portfolio of solution sets is then sent to all stakeholders.

Step #3. Team Uses Scorecards to Compare Design Solution Sets.

All stakeholders are then asked to review and rate each solution. They are asked to make judgments on both the *Ilities* and *Ings* of each design.

Each person must explain in detail the "why" of their position. These ratings and the accompanying comments are typically posted on the team's web site for review by all members of the project.

The design team uses these ratings and comments as an avenue for dialoging with stakeholders in regard to their concerns or suggestions.

The comments then become part of a growing database of knowledge. The classifications used in creating the *Lean Design Scorecards* make it easy for search engines to locate specific data across a wide range of projects.

Can Be Used At All Levels

Lean Design Scorecards are useful at all levels of product. The *Ility and Ing* equation applies universally at the System Level, Sub-System Level and Part Level.

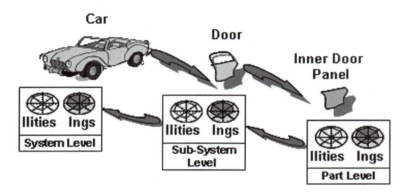

Lean Scorecards Used At All Levels

A team can agree on an overall *Ility* and *Ing* strategy for the System Level and then pass along their strategy to a Sub-System team. The Sub-System team can do the same for a team working at the product part level.

Lean Design Scorecards are also an effective way to share information and knowledge laterally between many teams working on a major project.

They can be used by management to assure all of the teams are aligned to the same strategic goals. They also enable management to review many designs without getting mired in the details.

Airline Seating Corporation (ASC) Scorecard Example

Following is a *Lean Design Scorecard* created by the imaginary American Seating Company (ASC) you met in Chapter Five. It describes the baseline for their new effort.

The darkened area is the "as is" of the existing seat. The scale used is 1-10 with a "10" indicating they are setting the standard for the industry.

The scale used is as follows:

Rating	Ility Value Level
9-10	Extremely High Value. Sets the standard for the industry
7-8	High Value. Superior to that of most competitors
5-6	Acceptable. Meets expectations most of the time
3-4	Low Value. Frequently does not meet expectations
1-2	Extremely Low Value. Well below that of all competitors

Note that the following *Strategic Ility Values* score a "4" or "Frequently does not meet expectations."

Featureability. Competitive seats offer value enhancing features in contrast to the ASC seat.

Deliverability. Aircraft Seating Company's deliveries are erratic due to the complexity of its product line offering.

Maintainability. High number of customer complaints about the degree of skill and amount of time required to service seats.

These low values typically become the primary targets the team will focus on first.

These eight *Strategic Ility Values* can then be broken down to a "*sub-Ility*" level for a better understanding of why the ratings are so low.

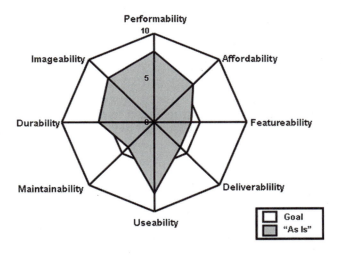

Ility Spider Chart Baseline

Causal Drivers of Poor Maintainabilty

The ASC team took a closer look at the reasons for the poor maintainability ratings.

They went to work applying the *Rule of the Onion.*

Based on the input of stakeholders and customers, they found four major reasons for the poor maintainability rating. (The scale used is the same as the one used for the *Strategic Ilities.*)

Replacement Part Availability (Rating = 5). Service parts sometimes out of stock due to complexity of many parts in the design.

Component Accessibility (Rating = 3). Current design makes it difficult to reach and replace parts.

High Adjustability (Rating = 3). Many adjustments required that need human skill and judgment.

Cleanability (Rating = 4). Very poor. Fabric materials used not easily cleanable.

The ASC team summarized the ratings for these four in the form of a *"sub-Ility"* chart with "Why?" commentary supporting each of the four legs.

The true nature of the ASC seat onion began to reveal itself.

Insert Artwork 6.5A here. "Maintainability Sub-Ility Chart"

The ASC team then went to work "peeling the onion" even more. They used the latest *Voice of the Customer* to work even more closely with customers to apply the *Rule of the Onion.*

Each sub-system was evaluated at to see if it was a major driver of the low "adjustability" rating.

Three sub-systems stood out as the culprits.

Following are their ratings and the "Why?" for each.

Adjustability Evaluation

Tray Table (Rating = 3). Adjustment required for both height and angle. Many complaints about variability of adjustment. Table considered to require too much maintenance time and skill.

Seat Bottom (Rating = 3). Seat bottom adjustment difficult to reach. Must be made "blind." Considerable discomfort for customer when out of adjustment. High priority serviceability issue.

Arm Rest (Rating = 3). Adjustment difficult to reach. Special tool needed to make the adjustment. Tool sometimes not available. No way to tell if adjustment properly done.

The ASC Team's *Rule of the Onion* evaluation revealed specific design challenges. It also revealed specific metrics that could be used to evaluate design solutions for each of these challenges.

Adjustability Metrics Become Clearer

Following are the metrics the ASC team considered to be the most important.

Also shown are some of the first ideas that emerged from their *Lean Design Kaizan* for solving these problems:

Metric	Description	Design Solutions?
Completion Time	Total time from problem identification to job completion.	Eliminate adjustments? Open accessibility to adjustments?
Skill Level	Level of skill based on a scale of 1-5. Lowest skill the goal.	Design for "a child can do it" level of skill?
Quality Assurance	Judgment level required to assure job done right.	Positive mechanical stops? No judgment required?
Tool Complexity	Number of standard tools. Number of special tools.	No tools? Standard tools only?

The ASC team "Peel the Onion" analysis described above gives all stakeholders a clear view of their thinking process.

It also gave stakeholders an opportunity to challenge the team as well as their own thoughts.

It made the current state of their knowledge *explicit* and *visible* to their entire team. It shows how the team plans to measure how well there are solving the first half of the Lean Design Equation:

Optimize Strategic Ilities,
Minimize Evil Ings

Here is how the ASC team's "Peel the Onion" process worked.

ASC Team Builds its Baseline Evil Ing Scorecard

Now the ASC team must go to work on creating a measurement system for the other side of the *Lean Design Scorecard.*

The same "Peel the Onion" approach is used.

However, this time the team uses the *Seven Evil Ings* to baseline the "as is" of the present ASC seat design.

The *Evil Ing* spider chart below shows what they discovered.

The darkened area is the baseline "as is" of the existing seat.

The scale used is 1-10 with a "1" indicating an extremely low amount of waste in a design. The amount is so low that it is well below that of all competitors.

The number "10" indicates an intolerable amount of product poor quality and waste. The amount is so high that it is setting the standard for the industry.

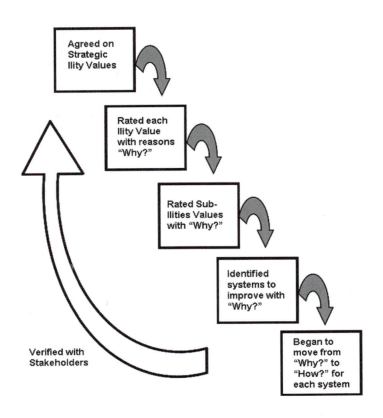

Note that the goal with the *Evil Ing* rating is to reduce the number to "1." The idea is to make the *darkened area smaller*.

The opposite is true for the *Strategic Ility Value* spider chart. Here the goal is to reach a "10" and make the darkened area larger.

The *Evil Ing* scale is as follows

Rating	Evil Ing Level
9-10	Intolerable. Highest level in the industry
7-8	Excessive. Worse than most competitors
5-6	Tolerable. High but controllable
3-4	Low. Minimum impact on cost and quality
1-2	Extremely Low. Well below that of all competitors

The ASC team went to work at their *Lean Design Kaizan* and came up with the following ratings for their current seat design and its *Seven Evil Ings*.

Each stakeholder from all the four product domains (*Design, Supply, Manufacture* and *Customer*) was asked to rate the present design from their perspective. For each of the *Seven Evil Ings*, they were also required to give their "whys?."

Here is what the team found.

The ASC team quickly discovered that many times all four domains were suffering from the same *Evil Ings* (for a definition of the *Seven Evil Ings*, revisit Chapter One).

Complexity (Rating = 8). The "whys?" showed that designers were spending most of their time on modifying designs. There was no standardization. Suppliers complained of many parts. The factory floor complained about many different processes.

And the customer domain was confused about the diversity and complexity of ordering a seat. The *Complexity Gremlin* was hard at work in the present design.

Precision (Rating = 7). The *Precision Gremlin* was also making his presence well known. The factory floor complained about excessively tight tolerances. Customers were upset about the precision required to adjust and maintain the seats.

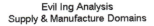

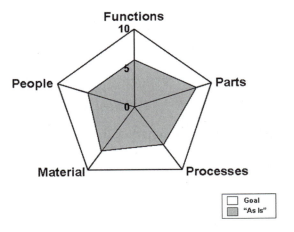

Variability (Rating = 5). Meanwhile, the *Variability Gremlin* was have a heyday with the 150 unique seat models in the ASC line. This was taxing engineering time as well as sales proposal time.

Sensitivity (Rating = 5). While the robustness level of the seat was tolerable, there were constant complaints about excessive seat wear. The *Sensitivity Gremlin* was hard at work. Airlines were extending cabin refits in order to reduce expense. The need was for new fabrics that could take a beating longer.

Immaturity (Rating = 2). The existing design certainly did not create the waste of being risky. Some designs were 10 years old. The *Immaturity Gremlin* was nowhere to be seen. In fact, the risk was that the existing seat design was too mature and competitors were moving out ahead of ASC.

Dangerous (Rating= 1). There was nothing about the existing seat, either in its manufacture or use, that created a danger to humans or the environment. In fact, the seat had very high ratings for safety performance. The *Dangerous Gremlin* had been all but eliminated by the ASC design team of a decade past.

High Skill (Rating = 7). It was the *Skill Gremlin* who was creating the most havoc. A high degree of skill was needed to make design modifications to the existing seat each time a new customer came on the scene.

Then there was the high level of manufacturing and assembly skill required to build the seat. This was followed by the skill level required for servicing the seat in the field, an issue the team had already discovered in their *Strategic Ility Scorecard* analysis.

Evil Ings in Manufacturing Domain

The ASC team's *Evil Ing* analysis revealed plenty of opportunity for solving the second half of the *Ility and Ing* equation:

Optimize Strategic Ilities,
Minimize Evil Ings

The team saw the greatest immediate opportunity was to take a closer look at how the *Seven Evil Ings* were attacking quality and cost in the Supply and Manufacturing Domains first.

They went to work applying the *Rule of the Onion* and its mandate to ask "why?" many times.

The team focused on the *Five Elements* that make up all products. They looked at how the cost and quality of these elements were being degraded by the *Seven Evil Ings*.

Based on the input of suppliers and their own manufacturing department, they found the following. The scale used is the same as that used for the *Seven Evil Ings* analysis shown above.

Following are their ratings and the "Why?" for each of the five:

Evil Ing Analysis: Supply and Manufacturing Domains

	Rating	"Why?"	Wasteful Ings
Functions	6	Every new seat order has a different set of functions. Very low commonality between styles.	Excessive stocking, handling, and inventorying at both suppliers and on manufacturing floor.
Parts	8	More than 1,500 unique part numbers. Shipment delays common.	Documenting, scheduling, tracking, inspecting, reworking, and handling.
Processes	6	Many processes highly variable. Many different processes used with low commonality.	Much part handling, tracking, validating, and certifying.
Material	7	Difficult to clean. Easy to soil or contaminate. Many different colors and styles.	Excessively high material scrapping, storing, fabric matching.
People	6	Very complex assembly process. High level of training required for seat testing and validation.	Recruiting, hiring, training, certifying, and retraining.

While an aggressive lean manufacturing effort had been going on at ASC for several years, it was running up against a wall. Most of the "low hanging fruit" had been picked.

It was becoming clearer and clearer that the complexity of the seat design itself had to be changed.

The *Evil Ing* scorecard analysis gave the ASC design team a way to systematically get to the root causes of the supply chain and factory floor problems.

ASC Moves from Problem to Solution

While the ASC analysis revealed specific design targets, it also gave them a way to begin the task of identifying specific metrics and design solutions.

Following are some metrics the ASC team considered to be the most important with some first cut ideas that emerged for solving these problems:

	Metrics	Design Solutions?
Functions	Number of special functions offered. Skill level and time required for "add on" functions.	Reduce and commonize number of functional features. Constrain special features to final line "add on" features.
Parts	Parts per basic "platform" seat. Parts requiring adjustment. Number of part numbers.	Build one platform seat. Use common parts across entire line. Restrict variability to color and modular final "add on" features.
Processes	Total number of manufacturing process types and steps. Process skill and variability levels.	Design to enable grouping of like processes on factory floor. Reduce and commonize process types used.
Material	Number of different fabric types and vendors required. Complexity of color selection.	Reduce fabric types used. Constrain variability to color selection.
People	Estimated manufacturing hours per seat. Skill levels for factory floor operations.	Use positive part identity to reduce floor quality problems. Design for lowest skill level possible.

The ASC team's "Peel the Onion" analysis described above gives all stakeholders a clear view of their thinking process. It also gave stakeholders an opportunity to challenge the team as well as contribute their own thoughts.

Like in the early *Ility Value* scorecard baseline analysis, it made the current state of their knowledge *visible to the entire team.*

Following are the steps the ASC team used in creating their *Evil Ing* scorecard.

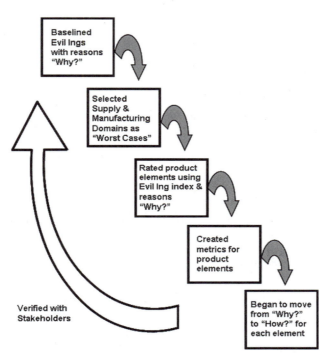

ASC Evil Ing Scorecard Process

Stakeholder and Management Buy-In

The ASC team's next task was to getting management participation and buy-in to their *Ility* and *Ing* Lean Design scorecard baselines.

The team did this during their management presentation immediately following their *Lean Design Kaizan*.

They knew never to launch a design without first gaining management's understanding of their basic product strategy. The result can be wasted time, weakened morale and squandered dollars.

The ASC team also knew their management was divided on the entire idea of developing a simplified "platform" seat.

Marketing management was especially concerned that airline customers would push back on this idea. Traditionally, airlines have used cabin color and seat design to differentiate their service from that of competitors.

However, manufacturing management was arguing that they were under severe pressure to reduce cost and the per unit cost. Their point was that the name of the game had shifted from *cabin feature* differentiation to *cost* differentiation.

The ASC team was careful to make sure all management points of view were in attendance at their post-*Kaizan* presentation. They wanted to use it as a step forward in getting management concurrence.

The *Lean Design Scorecard* baselines afforded a simple, clear structure for addressing product strategy issues.

During their presentation, the team was careful to show how their product strategy aligned with the company's overall business strategy.

After considerable debate and discussion both during their presentation and afterward, the ASC team got management buy-in to their design strategy and measurement system.

Management was unified in supporting their product strategy.

Set-Based Fast Feedback

The ASC team quickly used their new baseline scorecard as a way to evaluate new design solutions. They had a way to compare multiple solution sets without the problem of "apples to oranges."

Each new design was rated against the "as is" baseline.

The team knew that iterating many different design solutions before settling on one strategy is essential. This calls for the need to quickly compare one against another in order to find the best overall solution.

Fast feedback is essential for this type of *set-based design.*

The team also continued to refine their spider charts to add specific data for each *Ility Value* leg.

Management had a way to review many designs without having to "duck dive" into details.

Scorecards for each design could be digitally archived. Knowledge retrieval was easy by using simple search engines.

Knowledge decay was reduced.

Very importantly, all stakeholders had a way to participate in the ongoing design process. With each new design solution, they were asked to give their evaluation from their domain point of view.

This surfaced problems and opportunities with each new design early. It also strengthened knowledge sharing and stakeholder buy-in.

The *Ility and Ing* framework gave all stakeholders a common ground for sharing ideas.

Benefits of Lean Design Scorecards

The ASC team was asked to share their success in using their *Lean Design Scorecard* approach with the rest of the company. This is what they found:

Give Total View. The scorecards measured both value and waste concurrently. *Ility* and *Ing* metrics were at a high enough level to show the big picture but could be worked down to a low enough level to capture specific data. Scorecards give a *holistic* view.

Reveal Root Causes. The *Rule of the Onion* and the requirement to *ask why many times* enables the design team to understand a problem at the root cause level where they can do something about it.

Integrate Product Knowledge. Scorecards are useless without the participation of all company disciplines. They require the on-going participation of all stakeholders.

Enable Trade-Off Decisions. They give a way to look at many different designs in an orderly, logical way. Both quantitative and qualitative information can be used for making these trades.

Capture Knowledge. *Lean Design Scorecards* make it easy to archive and retrieve knowledge about design solutions and the reasons why — or why not — they were used. The use of spider charts makes the decisions highly visual.

Easy to Use. They are easy to create, understand and use. Scorecards provide a way to compare many different design solutions against a common set of corporate strategic objectives.

Why Toyota Excels in Knowledge Sharing

Toyota is now recognized as one of the world's best in lean product development. This is attributed in great part to their ability to practice "set based" design.

Toyota develops many different design solutions, reluctantly abandoning them until the final decision. Their goal is extended learning.

They also save these solutions for review during the next generation.

Toyota clearly recognizes that the loss of technical knowledge is one of the greatest wastes a company can suffer.

Discarded knowledge means lost capabilities. The time and money spent in developing these experiences are not the things lost. There is also the lost opportunity cost when we don't have the resources to answer a challenge.

Knowledge in any organization is most times informal, hidden and difficult to share. It resides in the minds of employees.

When it is made explicit or visible, most times it is disconnected. It resides in emails, bulletin boards, and data bases. The decentralization of the design process is making this knowledge disconnection even more complex.

Lean Design Scorecards offer a way to connect fragments of product knowledge.

They encourage individual experts to share their knowledge with a design team, and in so doing, share it with the organization.

Summary

- Good product design measurement is measuring what is important, not just what is easy to measure. *Lean Design Scorecards* give you a way to measure your design's potential for creating customer value and preventing lifecycle waste.
- A product design measurement system should do three things: (1) Make knowledge explicit and understandable, (2) Make that knowledge easy to communicate, and (3) Reduce the time to capture and retrieve that knowledge.
- The *Rule of the Onion* says you must peel back each layer and ask "why?" many times despite how many tears this causes. Design solutions must be directed at root causes.
- *Lean Design Scorecards* give all stakeholders an ongoing way to participate in the design process as it evolves. Buy-in to the final design decisions is incremental. Surprises are minimal.
- *Lean Design Scorecards* enable a design team to have fast feedback to emulate the Toyota practice called "set-based" design.

Addendum

Institute for Lean Design

The Institute for Lean Design offers training and coaching in the tools and techniques of the *Lean Design Solution*.

Certification is available both on-site and through webcast courses given by Bart Huthwaite.

Information is available at www.LeanDesign.org

How Lean Design Solution "Maps" To Other Tools

The tools and techniques in this book support existing product development tools now in use. The *Lean Design Solution* provides a framework for integrating existing methodologies.

	How *Lean Design Solution* Integrates…	Book Chapter and Tools
Design for Six Sigma (DFSS)	*Evil Ings* create framework for attacking root cause of poor quality	Chap. Four. How to prevent poor quality from taking root
Quality Function Deployment (QFD)	The *Eight Primary Customer Ilities* identify best values to deploy	Chap. Four. How to create your *Ility Value* strategy
Voice of the Customer (VOC)	*Ility and Ing Equation* gives framework for VOC in three time dimensions	Chap. Two. *Law of Marketplace Pull*
Value Stream Mapping (VSM)	*Lean Design Mapping* acts as front end tool for more detailed VSM	Chap. Five. *Lean Design Mapping Kaizan*
Design for Manufacture and Assembly (DFMA)	*Seven Essential Skills* gives basics for DFMA improvement	Chap. Four. *Lean Product Design Skills*
Phase/Toll Gate Reviews	*Lean Strategy Thinking* enables "seeing the whole before the parts"	Chap. Three. How to design your product delivery process
Set-Based Concurrent Engineering	*Law of Fast Feedback* way to quickly evaluate many designs	Chap. Four. How to create *Lean Design Scorecards*

Lean Design Lingo

Like all business languages, the lexicon of Lean Product Design is a mixture of many previous process languages, albeit with slightly different meanings, and some new terms.

Some of the words you will read here are directly from the lexicon of Lean Manufacturing. Others have emerged over the years as the practice of *Lean Product Solution* has spread to many companies.

Following are definitions of the major Lean Product Design terms.

Lean Design Equation. The fundamental equation all design teams must solve to create a truly lean design. This equation is expressed as *Optimize Strategic Ilities, Mimimize Evil Ings.* See Chapter One for a complete explanation of this equation.

The Five Laws of Lean Design. The five principles that govern solving the *Lean Design Equation.* These are (1) The Law of Strategic Value, (2) The Law of Waste Prevention, (3) The Law of Marketplace Pull, (4) The Law of Innovation Flow, and (5) The Law of Fast Feedback. See Chapter Two for a complete explanation of these.

Lean Design Champion. An individual or a team given the task of implementing Lean Product Design. Also used to describe a project team leader introducing lean design concepts to his design team. Also used by Black Belts to describe their role in training design teams in lean design practices.

Ility. Word used for a product attribute or value. Examples: manufacturability, marketability, maintainability and many more. The plural *Ilities* was first coined in 1985 by a John Deere design team to describe their product value strategy.

Primary Customer Ilities. The eight fundamental values all customers seek in a product. Lean Product Design uses these as a starting point for tailoring a product team's *value strategy* The *Eight Primary Customer Ilities* were first introduced by Bart Huthwaite at the Institute for Competitive Design (since renamed Institute for Lean Design) Annual Product Design and Development Conference on Mackinac Island, Michigan in 1991.

Primary Company Ilities. The eight fundamental attributes all companies want a product team to incorporate in their new product. The *Eight Primary Company Ilities* were the result of a multi-year study by the Institute for Competitive Design and were introduced at the same Mackinac Island conference noted above.

Ility Value Brothers. Cartoon characters used to bring to life the *Eight Primary Customer Values.* This good family helps design teams deliver the values all customers desire.

Ing. Word for any process, step or action required during a product's entire life cycle. Examples: testing, prototyping, machining, assembling, maintaining. This word first came into usage during a workshop at Rockwell Space Shuttle operations in 1986.

Good Ing. A process step that helps create product value. It has been argued that there is no such thing as a "good" *Ing* as all process steps are candidates for elimination by better design. The theoretical ideal number of *Ings* required for a product's life cycle value is zero.

Evil Ing. A process step that creates waste rather than product value. Classic examples are inspecting, storing, repairing, etc. A design team's challenge is to prevent these from ever happening by avoiding the use of the seven process types that create them.

Evil Ing Gremlins. Cartoon characters used to bring to life the seven types of design solutions that create most product life cycle waste. The *Evil Ing Gremlins* are the arch enemies of the good *Ility Brothers.* The term "gremlins" was widely used in England during World War II to describe the source of mechanical problems that bedeviled the famous Spitfire fighter plane.

Hidden Ings. Tasks or process steps that are difficult to predict and measure. Typically used to refer to indirect costs on the factory floor or unexpected tasks in the customer's domain. The lean manufacturing revolution's greatest gains are in reducing these kinds of indirect costs.

Visible Ings. Highly visible and quantifiable process steps such as machining and assembling. These are typically referred to as "direct costs."

Things. Word used to describe the physical integration of processes into parts. All parts are really combinations of processes. Coined by a Ford Motor engineer who said "The Ings" are really "Th-ings."

Evil Ing Busting. Term first used in 1996 to describe the systematic use of design tactics to prevent process complexity.

Lean Design Mapping (LDM). A systematic method developed by the Institute for Lean Design to create a lean product strategy, the first task of any design team.

Lean Design Kaizan. Intensive workshop used to start the process of improving or creating a new product design. *Lean Design Mapping (LDM)* is used as the primary focus of this *design kaizan.*

Lean Design Thinking. Used to describe the mental paradigm of optimizing value and minimizing waste throughout a product's lifecycle.

Lean Product Design Takt Time. The pace at which new products ideally flow to the customer. This means not over-reaching or under-delivering. All industries have historical *takt* times for absorbing new technology; however, these are shrinking.

Disruptive Takt Time Technology. The emergence of a new technology that radically changes the traditional process of innovation in an industry. Term originated with Clayton Christensen's book, *The Innovator's Dilemma.*

Lean Design Spider Charting. Practice of simultaneously measuring a product's predicted value and waste using "radar" or "spider charts". The purpose of such charting is to enable the comparison of alternative design solutions.

The Three Sharks of Change. Term used to describe the three forces of change that act on every design solution to assure its eventual demise. These are (1) New technology, (2) Marketplace preferences and (3) Competitive threats.

Muda. Japanese term for "waste." Typically used by lean manufacturing practitioners to describe factory floor waste.

Super Muda. Term coined to describe waste in customer's domain created by poor design. This type of waste can result in the greatest waste of all, the loss of a customer.

Lean Opportunity Domains. The four primary product life cycle phases. These are (1) Design, (2) Supply, (3) Manufacture, and (3) Customer Use. Lean Product Design attempts to create value and prevent waste in all four.

Five Lean Targets. The five major elements of all products that can be improved with better design. These five are: (1) Product functions, (2) Parts, (3) Lifecycle processes, (4) Materials (including consumables) and (5) People.

The Eight Top Lean Tactics. The eight most used lean design techniques. See Chapter Four for a description of these.

The 22 Most Valuable Lean Design Team Rules

Rules Lean Design Teams have taught me and how you can profit by them

Where Did These Rules Originate? These rules were collected from product design teams around the world. For the past two decades, I have added new ones each year to my growing collection.

What follows are the 22 most frequently used.

Why Rules? Rules set boundaries and focus energy. Project teams welcome rules, especially when they have a role in setting them. The following rules will both establish your leadership as well as enable your team to move ahead rapidly.

How to Use These Rules: Offer these rules to your team as a "code of conduct." Don't push these down your team's throats. Don't adopt any rule where there is not 100 percent agreement. Immediately encourage your team to start adding more rules.

1. Rule of Urgency

Never finish a lean design task on time. Urgency breeds action. Always strive to finish ahead of time. Build a constant sense of urgency and enthusiasm.

Tip: Always have a large clock in full view in your meeting room. Don't use your watch and be the "time cop." A clock on the wall is an impartial keeper of time.

Set time limits, no matter how small the task. Time limits create intensity and squeeze out waste. Deadlines help get jobs done. Time is your most precious resource. Use it wisely.

Tip: Remember that work typically expands to fill time. Reducing time focuses team effort and helps drive out wasteful effort.

2. Rule of *Strategic Ilities*

Strategic Ilities are values that will delight your customer and differentiate your product. Examples are affordability, serviceability, performability, etc.

Tip: Find and focus on the strategic few that will make your product a success. Typically six to eight Ilities will determine your ultimate success.

3. Rule of *Evil Ings*

Evil Ings are the wasteful process steps used during a product's life-cyle to deliver the values or *Ilities*.

Evil Ings are set in motion by seven types of design solutions having excessive (1) complexity, (2) precision, (3) variability, (4) sensitivity, (5) immaturity, (6) danger, and (7) skill.

These types of design solutions create wasteful tasks such as storing, inspecting, maintaining, fixing, etc.

Tip: The universal design rule must always be Optimize Strategic Ilities, Minimize Evil Ings.

4. Rule of the Titanic

Know where the icebergs are before you ever leave the dock. Seek out potential design problems early. You will never solve a problem you don't know exists.

Surface expectations, concerns, obstacles, and agendas early. Get potential problems out in the open quickly.

Tip: Task your team to write down their expectations and concerns at the very start of your project. Don't try to answer them immediately. Post them in full view and promise that each one will be addressed during the course of your project.

5. Rule of Individual Thought First

Ask for individual thought first, group discussion second. Your goal is to encourage total participation. Have your team members quietly write down their own thoughts and then share them with the team.

Tip: Use Yellow stickies (Post It Notes) to make abstract ideas "real" and create ownership. They can also be easily grouped into families of ideas.

6. Rule of Diversity

Seek diverse views, especially at the start of your project, from all "stakeholders." Surface as many ideas and problems as possible. Go problem seeking before problem solving.

Tip: You can always reconfigure or reduce the size of your team later. Build broad ownership right from the start.

7. Rule of the Stakeholders

Involve all those who must help implement your project right at the start. They will understand the problem, "own" the project, and help you deliver your solutions later.

8. Rule of Divide and Discover

When you are challenged with a tough problem, spark innovation by dividing your team into sub-teams, all working the same challenge at the same time. The number of new and different ideas will amaze you.

Why? Smaller groups improve the opportunity for deeper thought and discussion. Sharing ideas among multiples teams reveals new ideas and reveals common themes or problems.

Reasons: Especially try this at the beginning of your project. Smaller groups improve discussion. Sharing ideas among sub-teams reveals common themes, more ideas.

9. Rule of the Customer's Voice

Beware of the customer's voice. It seldom tells the "real" truth. Listen to it with caution. Always remember to try and hear the voice of the "non-customer."

Customers typically speak in the "present tense." They describe what they would like different today and, most times, don't do a very good job of expressing their real needs.

Your challenge is to discover these unspoken needs as well as to understand their future needs, the ones that will keep you "ahead of the pack."

Tip: Encourage your customer to predict what he will need in the future.

10. Rule of Iteration

Never go for the 100 percent solution immediately. Leave room to revisit the problem. You will never get it exactly right the first time.
Tip: First solutions are typically sub-optimal solutions.

11. Rule of the Two Project Skills

Great projects are as much a social science as a technical science.
You must apply two skills at the same time: (1) Technical Skill — What we will deliver and (2) Human Skill — How we will work with our customer, our management and among ourselves as a team.

11. Rule of Inertia

A body at rest tends to stay at rest. Get your project team into motion fast. It's tough to steer a parked car.

12. Rule of Common Ground

Build your lean product team on a solid foundation of agreement. When doing tasks, agree on what you can agree on and then move on.
Tip: Put tough issues into a "parking lot" to be revisited later. Don't get "wrapped around the axle." You will be surprised by how many tough issues begin to disappear when the focus is on agreement, not disagreement.

13. Rule of Decision-Making

Decide on your decision-making processes before you must use them. Remember the three major ones: mandate, ballot and consensus and use them appropriately.

14. Rule of Precision

Excessive precision in any project, product or service is evil. Seek robust solutions.
Why: Precision demands high skill, close supervision and, when it is not within control, can result in costly re-work.
Eliminate precision by opening tolerances and using processes that don't require close control.

15. Rule of Project Chaos

When working on too many problems at the same time, something is bound to go terribly wrong.

Tip: Avoid complex solutions where the failure of one step can have a disastrous effect on your entire project.

16. Rule of the Three Sharks

Three forces of change will constantly attack your lean solutions. They are: (1) Marketplace, (2) Competition and (3) Technology. All product designs competitively degrade over time.

Make sure you know where they are now as well as where they might be in the future, or risk being eaten alive. Staying ahead of all three is the key to survival.

17. Rule of Step, Stretch and Leap

Think about your project in three time dimensions: Step — Solutions for the present; Stretch — Solutions for the mid-term or next generation, and Leap — Solutions for the long term or distant future.

Why: This kind of multi-generational thinking can prevent you from having to "reinvent the wheel" in the future. This kind of thinking will prepare you for the future before it arrives.

It will also help you develop technology off-line and, hopefully, ahead of the competition.

18. Rule of Early Wins

Go for some quick wins. They build team morale, strengthen management buy-in and improve customer confidence.

Fact: Early wins build momentum for success. Document these successes, no matter how minor. The old adage "seeing is believing" holds true today.

19. Rule of the Itch

Find your customer's most immediate "itch" and quickly scratch it. You will move to the head of the line for all other itches that will arise.

Tip: Smart lean product teams quickly identify the most immediate concerns and needs of their stakeholders. They satisfy these first to quickly build confidence and trust.

20. Rule of Measurement

Remember "what gets measured gets done." However, measure first to improve your lean product, not to just "prove" a point.

More Rules of Project Measurement:

Measure what is important, not just what is easy to measure
Measure in real time, so you still have time for corrective action
Measure for direction first, precision second
Measure all project objectives concurrently
Measure visually

Enable those who will be measured to help create the measurements.

21. Rule of Systems Thinking

Always remember that a project solution depends more on how each solution interacts with other solutions, rather than on how these solutions act independently.

When one project solution is improved independently of another, the total project solution can begin to lose its overall efficiency.

22. The Final Rule of Rules

Enable those who must abide by the rules to help write them. They will better understand them and abide by them.

Rules imposed arbitrarily from "on high" are seldom faithfully followed.

Lean Product Design Bookshelf

Beckwith, Harry, *Selling the Invisible*, Warner Books.

Brown, Mark Graham, *Keeping Score: Using the Right Metrics to Drive World-Class Performance*, Quality Resources, New York, New York. 1996.

Case, John, *The Open-Book Experience: Lessons from Over 100 Companies Who Successfully Transformed Themselves*, Addison-Wesley, Reading, Mass. 1998.

Chang, Richard Y. and Paul De Young, *Measuring Organizational Improvement Impact*, Richard Chang Associates, Inc., Publications Division, Irvine, California 1996.

Christensen, Clayton M. and Michael E. Raynor, *The Innovator's Solution: Creating and Sustaining Successful Growth*, Harvard Business School Press, Boston, 2003.

Christensen, Clayton M., *The Innovator's Dilemma*, Harvard Business School Press, Boston, 1997.

Cooper, Robert G. *Winning at New Products: Accelerating the Process from Idea to Launch*, Cambridge, MA: Perseus Publishing, Third Edition, 2001.

> *This book is the classic in the field of phase gate product development. Cooper calls his process Stage-Gate™ a systematic way to shepherd a product from concept to customer. The first edition was published in 1986.*

Cross, Nigel. *Engineering Design Methods: Strategies for Product Design*, Third Edition, John Wiley & Sons, Ltd. 2000.

> *I consider this book by far the best I have ever read on the art of mechanical design. Cross explores the true nature of the design process. He gives a clear, succinct description of design tasks and tools. He then ends with a good rationale for all design teams creating a design strategy. The book is now used as a standard text in many U.K. universities. My first edition is well worn as I have returned to it many times for advice.*

de Holan, Pablo Martin, Nelson Phillips and Thomas B. Lawrence, "Managing Organizational Forgetting," *MIT Sloan Management Review,* Winter 2004, Vol. 45, No. 2, pp. 45-51.

Insightful article on the failure of companies to capture and re-use organizational knowledge.

Drucker, Peter, "The Discipline of Innovation," Harvard Business Review on The Innovative Enterprise, Harvard Business School Press, Boston, 2003

Fast Company, "Masters of Design: 20 Creative Mavericks and What You Can Learn From Them," June 2004, pp. 61-75

Gause, Donald C. and Gerald M. Weinberg, *Are Your Lights On? How to Figure Out What the Problem Really Is,* New York: Dorset House Publishing.

First published in 1982 and now a classic, this little book addresses the many encountered in the art of problem solving. Offering such insights as "A problem is a difference between things as desired and things as perceived," the authors look at ways to improve one's thinking power. Gause and Weinberg's approach corresponds with the Lean Design Strategy Mapping steps #1 to #4 of identifying and understanding the design problem before beginning the task of solving it. A good read for shaking up old paradigms.

Harvard Business Review on The Innovative Enterprise, Harvard Business School Press, Boston, 2003.

A paperback incorporating eight articles by leading thinkers on innovation theory and practice taken from the Harvard Business Review. A good, quick read.

Hirshberg, Jerry, *The Creative Priority: Driving Innovative Business in the Real World.* New York: Harper Business.Leonard, Dorothy. *Wellsprings of Knowledge: Building and Sustaining the Sources of Innovation,* Harvard Business School Press, year of publication?

The author shows why some companies are better at managing innovation than others. This book gives excellent examples of both successes and failures in new product development. This is a good book for a lean design champion who has the task of helping to build a more innovative product development process. See Leonard's Chapter 4, p. 92 for how best to tackle the problem of implementing and integrating new technical processes and tools.

Leonard, Dorothy and Walter Swap, *When Sparks Fly: Igniting Creativity in Groups*, Harvard Business School Press, year of publication?

The authors dispel the notion that creativity is limited to rare individuals or only highly creative groups. Leonard and Swap give strategies for stimulating more creativity in teams. They maintain that any group can be more creative, even if its members individually would not score highly on tests for creativity. This book is a good source for lean design champions who are looking for ways to energize their lean design team's creative juices.

Levitt, Theodore, "Creativity Is Not Enough" in *Harvard Business Review on The Innovative Enterprise*, Harvard Business School Press, pp. 155-179, 2003

Levitt takes dead aim at the assumption that creativity is superior to conformity in business. By failing to take into account practical matters of implementation, big thinkers can inspire organizational cultures dedicated to "abstract chatter" rather than purposeful action.

Lynch, Richard L. and Kelvin F. Cross, *Measure Up! Yardsticks for Continuous Improvement*, Basil Blackwell, Inc., Cambridge, Mass., 1991.

McGrath, Michael. *Setting the Pace® In Product Development: A Guide to Product and Cycle Time Excellence®*, Newton, MA: Butterworth-Heinemann, 1996.

Edited by the founding director of Pittiglio Rabin Todd & McGrath (PRTM), a leading U.S. product development consulting firm, this book describes what PRTM calls "Product And Cycle-time Excellence (PACE), a way for organizing a product development enterprise-wide process. This is an excellent book for understanding the major elements of a successful product development process and what each element must deliver. It is good, well-written "holistic" overview for lean design champions.

Nadler, Gerald and Hibino, Shozo. *Breakthrough Thinking: Why We Must Change the Way We Solve Problems, And the Seven Principles to Achieve This.*

One of my favorite books on problem solving. Their "Solution After Next" Principle addresses the need for thinking ahead to the next problem. Nadler and Hibino see all solutions, no matter how ideal they may seem at the time, as merely transitional steps. They say people have been conditioned by conventional problem solving to expect an entire change to be made all at once and then to be complete.

O'Connor, Kevin with Paul D. Brown, *The Map of Innovation: Creating Something Out of Nothing,* Random House, New York, 2003.

Pahl, G. and W. Beitz, English translation edited by Ken Wallace. *Engineering Design: A Systematic Approach,* Springer-Verlag, Berlin, 1996.

Written by two of Europe's leading experts on product design, this lengthy tome (544 pages) is a concise, comprehensive, clear approach to what the authors call "systematic engineering design." This book is definitely for the serious lean design champion who wants to dive deeply into the intricacies of the total design process.

Rath & Strong, *Design for Six Sigma Pocket Guide,* Lexington, MA: Rath & Strong Publishing, First Edition, 2002.

Reinertsen, Donald G., *Managing the Design Factory: A Product Developer's Toolkit,* The Free Press, New York, 1997.

Robinson, Alan G. and Sam Stern, *Corporate Creativity: How Innovation and Improvement Actually Happen,* Berrett-Koehler Publishers, Inc., San Francisco, 1997.

Outlines the six elements of corporate creativity which play a role in every creative act: Alignment, Self-Initiated activity, Unofficial activity, Serendipity, Diverse stimuli, and Within Company communication.

Rosenau, Jr., Milton D, Abbie Griffin, George A. Castellion, and Ned F. Anschuetz, *PDMA Handbook of New Product Development,* John Wiley & Sons, Inc., New York, 1996. *Some 33 chapters writ-*

ten by NPD professionals all aspects of new product development. A comprehensive, valuable addition for the serious practitioner's library.

Rubinstein, Moshe F. and Iris R.Firstenberg, *The Minding Organization: Bring the Future to the Present and Turn Creative Ideas into Business Solutions,* John Wiley & Sons, New York, 1999.

Slywotzky, Adrian and Richard Wise with Karl Weber, ,*How to Grow When Markets Don't,* Warner Books, New York, 2003.

Trout, Jack. *Trout on Strategy: Capturing Mindshare, Conquering Markets,* McGraw-Hill, New York, 2004.

Great for bite sized common sense ideas that are not so common. Trout is a well-known marketing strategy guru.

Trout, Jack with Steve Rivkin, *The Power of Simplicity: A Management Guide to Cutting Through the Nonsense and Doing Things Right,* McGraw-Hill, New York, 1999.

Utterback, James M. *Mastering the Dynamics of Innovation: How Companies Can Seize Opportunities in the Face of Technological Change.* Harvard Business School Press, Boston, 1994.

A deep well of stories about industrial innovation from the birth of the typewriter to the emergence of personal computers, from gas lamps to fluorescent lighting, from George Eastman's amateur photography to electronic imaging. Utterback asserts that existing organizations must consistently embrace innovation, even when it appears to undermine traditional strengths. This book is a gold mine of stories a lean product champion can use to make his point about aggressive innovation

VonOech, Roger, *A Whack on the Side of the Head: How You Can Be More Creative* (New York: Warner Books, 1990) and *A Kick In The Seat Of The Pants* (New York: Harper & Row, 1986).

Ward, Allen C. *The Lean Development Skills Book,* Ward Synthesis, Inc., First Edition, 2002.

Womack, James P. and Daniel T.Jones, *Lean Thinking: Banish Waste and Create Wealth in Your Corporation,* Free Press, New York, 2003.

Zook, Chris. *Beyond the Core: Expand Your Market Without Abandoning Your Roots,* Harvard Business School Press, Boston, 2004.

Zook argues that the best companies fuel sustained growth through carefully planned "adjacency moves" — expansion into areas away from but related to their core business.

About the Author

Bart Huthwaite, Founder, Institute for Lean Design, has coached engineers and design teams in new project and product development at more than **1000 companies** over the past **22 years.**

Bart's **Lean Six Sigma Product Design** tools and techniques are now being used to develop both *lean products* as well as *better quality products and services..*

He has deep experience in New Product Development, Design for Manufacture & Assembly, Design for Six Sigma, Design for Simplicity, Design to Cost, Integrated Product & Process Design, Concurrent Engineering, and other design techniques.

He is the founder of the **Institute for Lean Design** and creator of **Lean Design Mapping.** He is also the founder of two companies, the last of which was purchased by **Nitto Seiko** of Japan.

He is the author of *Engineering Change,* a "how to" guide for re-inventing your product development process, *Strategic Design,* a step-by-step road map for product teams, and *Concurrent Engineering User's Guide,* which answers the questions most asked by multi-functional product teams. Bart's latest book is *The Lean Design Solution: A Practical Guide to Streamlining Product Design and Development.* Bart is a powerful, creative speaker who champions lean product design at major conferences and management meetings worldwide.

Clients include Motorola, Microsoft, Siemens, Johnson & Johnson, ABB, Textron, Ford Motor, SKF, John Deere, EDS, Caterpillar, Siemens, Ericsson, Lockheed Martin, General Dynamics, 3M, Allied Signal, Whirlpool, ITT, Gulfstream Aerospace, US Navy and hundreds more in the telecommunications, automotive, aerospace and other fields worldwide.

Bart Huthwaite can be reached at:

Institute for Lean Design
9 French Outpost
PO Box 1999
Mackinac Island, Michigan 49757

www.LeanDesign.org
Tel: 906 847-6094
Fax: 906 847-6047
E-mail: huthwaite@aol.com